To

_____

From

_____

Date

_____

Mini Devotions: The Power of Prayer
Published by Christian Art Publishers
PO Box 1599, Vereeniging, 1930, RSA

© 2019
First edition 2019

Devotions compiled from *One-Minute Devotions® The Power of Prayer*

Cover designed by Christian Art Publishers

Designed by Christian Art Publishers

Images used under license from Shutterstock.com

Unless otherwise indicated, all Scripture quotations are taken from the
Holy Bible, New International Version®, NIV® Copyright
© 1973, 1978, 1984 by Biblica, Inc.® Used by permission.
All rights reserved worldwide.

Scripture quotations marked NLT are taken from the Holy Bible,
New Living Translation, copyright © 1996, 2004 by Tyndale House
Foundation. Used by permission of Tyndale House Publishers,
Carol Stream, Illinois 60188. All rights reserved.

Scripture quotations marked NKJV are taken from the New King James
Version®. Copyright © 1979, 1980, 1982 by Thomas Nelson, Inc.
Used by permission. All rights reserved.

Printed in China

ISBN 978-1-4321-3138-8

21 22 23 24 25 26 27 28 29 30 – 14 13 12 11 10 9 8 7 6 5

MINI DEVOTIONS

THE

POWER

of

★ ★ ★

Prayer

E.M. BOUNDS

CHRISTIAN ART
PUBLISHERS

Prayer that Gets Results

"I tell you the truth, if anyone says to this
mountain, 'Go, throw yourself into the sea,' and
does not doubt in his heart but believes that
what he says will happen, it will be done for him."

Mark 11:23

Genuine, authentic faith must be free of doubt. It is
not a mere belief in the being, goodness and power
of God – there's more to it than that. Through faith
and prayer, God's promises will be done.

Our major concern is our faith – its growth and
its tidings brought forth through its development.
A faith that holds on to the very things it asks for,
without doubt or fear.

We need this type of faith in our prayers.

ALMIGHTY GOD, I pray that You will grant
me genuine, authentic faith which believes that
anything is possible with You. Amen.

Being Sure

Faith is being sure of what we hope for
and certain of what we do not see.

Hebrews 11:1

Faith determines our relationship with God – how
we deal with Him and how we see Him as the
Savior. Faith grabs hold of the truth in God's Word
and is energized and inspired by His holy fire.

God is the great objective of faith, for faith rests
its whole weight on His Word. Faith is not an aimless
act of the soul, but a looking to God and trusting in
His promises. Faith is not believing just *anything*. It is
believing God, resting in Him and trusting His Word.

FATHER GOD, it is my desire to be conscious of
You all the time. Please increase my faith so that I
will look to You and rest in Your promises. Amen.

— **3** —

A Life of Good Report

These were all commended for their faith, yet
none of them received what had been promised.

Hebrews 11:39

Today, many believers obtain a good report because
of their donations and their gifts and talents. But
there are few who obtain a good report because of
their great faith or great prayer life. Today, as much
as at any time, we need followers of God to have
great faith and powerful prayer.

These are the two most important virtues that
make men great in the eyes of God. These two things
create spiritual success in the life and work of the
church. It should be our main concern to see that we
keep this kind of quality faith before God.

DEAR LORD, I want to live a life of good
report. Please help and guide me in developing a
life of great faith and prayer for Your glory. Amen.

Humility

Do not think of yourself more highly than
you ought, but rather think of yourself with
sober judgment, in accordance with the
measure of faith God has given you.

Romans 12:3

Happy are those who have no goodness of their own
to boast of. Humility flourishes in the soil of a true
and deep sense of our own insignificance. Nowhere
does humility flourish so as when it admits all guilt,
confesses all sin, and trusts all grace.

"I the chief of sinners am, but Jesus died for me."
That is the praying ground, the ground of humility,
but in reality brought near by the blood of the Lord
Jesus Christ. God dwells in the lowly places. He
makes lowly places often the most high places to the
praying soul.

★　★　★

LORD GOD, "I the chief of sinners am, but Jesus
died for me." Thank You that we can know that
when we humble ourselves before You, You will
lift us up. Amen.

Twin Enemies of Faith

So do not throw away your confidence;
it will be richly rewarded.

Hebrews 10:35

Doubt and fear are twin enemies of faith. Sometimes they actually take the place of faith, and although we continue to pray, it is a restless, disquieted, uneasy prayer that we offer. But doubts and fears should never be accommodated.

We must take our eyes off ourselves. They should be removed from our own weakness and allowed to rest fully on God's strength. A simple, confiding faith, living day by day, will drive fear away. Faith is able to cast your burdens onto God and not feel anxious about the outcome.

DEAR LORD, doubt and fear often threaten our faith. I want to thank You for delivering us when we bring our weaknesses, doubts and fears before You in prayer. Amen.

Humility Gives Wings to Prayer

Be completely humble and gentle;
be patient, bearing with one another in love.

Ephesians 4:2

Humility does not have its eyes on self, but rather on God and others. God puts a great price on humility of heart. That which brings the praying soul near to God is humility of heart. That which gives wings to prayer is a humble mind.

Pride, self-esteem, and self-praise effectually shut the door of prayer. Approach God with humility and meekness – do not be puffed up with self-importance or overestimate your virtues and good works. It is better to be clothed with humility than with an expensive garment.

FATHER GOD, You put a great price on humility. Please give me a humble and gentle heart so that my soul may draw ever closer to You. In Jesus' name. Amen.

The Divine Cure for Fear

Do not be anxious about anything,
but in everything, by prayer and petition,
with thanksgiving, present your requests to God.

Philippians 4:6

This Scripture verse describes the divine cure for all fear, anxiety, and worry. All these things are closely related to doubt and unbelief. This Scripture verse is also the divine prescription for securing the peace that surpasses all understanding and keeps the heart and mind in quietness and peace.

We need to guard against unbelief as we would against an enemy. Faith needs to be cultivated. Faith is increased by exercise; by being put to use. It is nourished by trials.

Faith grows by reading and meditating on the Word of God. Most of all, faith thrives in an atmosphere of prayer.

DEAR LORD GOD, thank You that Your Word so clearly assures us that we need not worry or fear. You are always in control. Amen.

A Great Work

In his pride the wicked does not seek Him;
in all his thoughts there is no room for God.

Psalm 10:4

It was said that Augustus Caesar found Rome a city of wood and left it a city of marble. The pastor who succeeds in changing his congregation from non-prayers, to prayer-filled people, has done a greater work than Augustus did. This is the major work of the preacher.

His main business is to turn people from being forgetful about God, into people who habitually pray, believe in God, and do His will. The preacher is not sent simply to get them to do better. He is sent to get them to pray, to trust God, and to keep their eyes on God.

GOD ALMIGHTY, I want to do great work for Your Kingdom. Thank You that I only need to plant a tiny seed; You will water it. Amen.

Saved by Faith

For it is by grace you have been saved, through faith.

Ephesians 2:8

The work of the ministry is to change unbelieving sinners into praying, believing saints. The value of faith cannot be disputed. God has placed tremendous importance and value on faith and that is why we need faith in order to be saved. So, when we think about the great importance of prayer, we find faith standing right beside it.

By faith we are saved, and by faith we *stay* saved. Prayer introduces us to a life of faith. Paul declared that the life he lived, he lived by faith in the Son of God who loved him and gave Himself for him. Therefore, Paul walked by faith and not by sight.

DEAR GOD, thank You that I, like Paul, may also live a life of faith in Your Son who loves me and who gave Himself for my sins. Amen.

Faith's Inseparable Companion

Anyone who comes to Him must
believe that He exists and that He rewards
those who earnestly seek Him.

Hebrews 11:6

Prayer is absolutely dependent on faith. Prayer accomplishes nothing unless it is connected to faith. Faith makes prayer effective and must precede it.

Before we even start to pray, our faith should be working. We must have faith that God is a rewarder of those who diligently seek His face.

This is the primary step in praying. While faith does not bring the blessing, it puts prayer in a position to ask for it. It leads to another step of understanding by helping the petitioner believe that God is able and willing to bless.

★　★　★

LORD JESUS, without faith our prayers are without effect. Thank You that faith puts prayer in action. I praise Your name. Amen.

God Rewards

"Your Father, who sees what is
done in secret, will reward you."

Matthew 6:4

Faith opens the way for prayer to approach God. But it also does more. It accompanies prayer with every step. When requests are made to God, faith turns the asking into obtaining. Prayer can help build your faith, which will produce results.

Faith makes prayer strong and gives it patience to wait on God. Faith believes that God rewards. No truth is more clearly revealed and none is more encouraging in Scripture than this. Serving God – no matter how insignificant it may seem – will yield a reward. That is what faith whole-heartedly believes. Faith gives its hearty consent to this precious truth.

FATHER, thank You that even the most insignificant service done in Your name will surely receive its reward. Glory to Your name. Amen.

Do Not Grow Weary

I want men everywhere to lift up holy
hands in prayer, without anger or disputing.

1 Timothy 2:8

Doubting is always forbidden because it stands as an enemy to faith and hinders effective prayer. Paul gives us conditions for successful prayer.

All questioning must be guarded against and avoided. Faith must banish doubt.

Great incentives to prayer are furnished in Scripture. Our Lord closes His teaching about prayer with the assurance and promise of heaven. The presence of Jesus Christ in heaven and the preparation He is making there for His saints help us not to grow weary in prayer.

★ ★ ★

LORD, please drive away the doubts and fear in my life that hinders my prayers and threatens my faith. I ask this in Jesus' name. Amen.

The Spirit of a Pilgrim

But those who hope in the LORD will
renew their strength. They will soar on
wings like eagles; they will run and not grow
weary, they will walk and not be faint.

Isaiah 40:31

The assurance that the Lord will come again to receive His saints strengthens and sweetens our difficult work on earth! To know that God is preparing a place for us in heaven is the star of hope to prayer. It is the wiping away of tears and putting the sweet odor of heaven into the bitterness of life.

The spirit of a pilgrim makes praying easier. An earthbound, earth-satisfied spirit cannot pray. The flame of spiritual desire in such a heart has gone out. The wings of its faith are clipped, its eyes are glazed over and its tongue is silenced. But they who wait continually upon the Lord *do* renew their strength!

GOD, only You can sweeten the bitterness of life and change my tears to laughter. I wait on You; You will renew my strength. Amen.

Modesty

Honor one another above yourselves.

Romans 12:10

To be humble is to have a low estimate of oneself. Humility retires itself from the public gaze. It does not seek publicity, neither does it care for prominence. It never exalts itself in the eyes of others or even in the eyes of itself. Modesty is one of its most prominent characteristics.

In humility there is the total absence of pride, and it is far-removed from anything like self-conceit. There is no self-praise in humility. Rather, it has the disposition to praise others. It is willing to take the lowliest seat and prefers those places where it will be unnoticed. Humility is meek behavior, a submissive spirit and a modest heart.

DEAR FATHER GOD, I know that it is only through Your grace I have been saved. Please grant me a submissive spirit and a modest heart. Amen.

A Rare Christian Grace

Be completely humble and gentle;
be patient, bearing with one another in love.

Ephesians 4:2

Humility is a rare Christian grace of great price in the courts of heaven, and is necessary for effective prayer. It provides access to God when other qualities fail. Its full portrait is found only in the Lord Jesus Christ. Our prayers must be set low before they can ever rise high.

In our Lord's teaching humility has such prominence and is such a distinguishing feature of His character, that to leave it out of His lesson on prayer would be wrong. It would deny a very important aspect of God's character.

DEAR LORD JESUS, I want to be more like You every day. Please grant me the rare Christian grace of humility so that everyone may see You in me. Amen.

A Praying Pharisee

"I tell you that this man, rather than
the other, went home justified before God.
For everyone who exalts himself will be humbled,
and he who humbles himself will be exalted."

Luke 18:14

The parable of the Pharisee and tax collector stands out in such bold relief. The Pharisee seemed to be accustomed to prayer. Certainly he should have known by that time how to pray. He left business and business hours and walked with steady and fixed steps up to the house of prayer. The position and place were well chosen by him.

But this praying ecclesiastic, though schooled in prayer by training and by habit, does not really pray. Words are uttered by him, but words are not prayer. That season of temple going has had no worship in it whatsoever.

O FATHER, I don't want my prayers to be like that of the Pharisee. I want to come before Your throne with an honest and humble heart. Amen.

A Praying Tax Collector

"But the tax collector stood at a distance. He would
not even look up to heaven, but beat his breast
and said, 'God, have mercy on me, a sinner.'"

Luke 18:13

The tax collector, guilt-ridden with a deep sense
of his wrong doings and his sinfulness, falls down
with humiliation before God with cries for mercy. A
sense of sin and of utter unworthiness have fixed the
humility deep down in his soul. This is the picture of
humility as opposed to pride in praying.

Here we see, by sharp contrast, the utter worth-
lessness of self-praise in praying. We see the beauty
and the divine praise that comes to humility of heart,
self-depreciation and self-condemnation when a soul
comes before God in prayer.

LORD, I don't want to pray worthless prayers of
self-praise. I pray with the tax collector, "God, have
mercy on me, a sinner." Amen.

Humility Loves Obscurity

This happened that we might not rely on
ourselves but on God. He has delivered us
from such a deadly peril, and He will deliver
us. On Him we have set our hope.

2 Corinthians 1:9-10

Humility is an indispensable requisite of true prayer. Humility must be in the praying character as light is in the sun.

Humility is born by looking at God and His holiness, and then looking at self and man's unholiness. Humility loves obscurity and silence, esteems the virtues of others, excuses their faults with mildness and easily pardons injuries. It knows the riches of the cross and the humiliations of Jesus Christ.

By approaching God's throne in humility, a person will find comfort in knowing that God is all-powerful. Humility strives to be holy, like God is holy.

DEAR GOD, please grant me humility, and then recognizing my own sinfulness. Thank You for Your amazing grace. Amen.

The Pride of Doing

"Many will say to Me on that day, 'Lord, Lord, did we not prophesy in Your name, and in Your name drive out demons and perform many miracles?' Then I will tell them plainly, 'I never knew you. Away from Me, you evildoers!'"

Matthew 7:22-23

Humility is the first and last attribute of Christ-like religion and the first and last attribute of Christ-like praying. There is no Christ without humility.

How graceful and imperative does the attitude of humility become to us! Humility is an unchanging attitude of prayer. Pride sends its poison all through our praying. The same pride infects all our prayers, no matter how beautifully worded they may be.

This lack of humility, this self-applauding, kept the most religious man of Christ's day from being accepted by God. The same thing will keep us today from being accepted by God.

DEAR FATHER, create in me a pure heart and renew a humble spirit within me. Amen.

The Business of Prayer

We will give our attention to
prayer and the ministry of the Word.

Acts 6:4

The apostles knew the necessity and worth of prayer to their ministry. They knew that their high commission as apostles – instead of relieving them from the necessity of prayer – committed them to it even more.

They were exceedingly jealous when other important work exhausted their time and prevented them from praying as they ought. As a result, they appointed laymen to do the jobs that were distracting them from their prayer time.

Prayer is put first. They made a business of it, surrendering themselves to praying, putting fervor, urgency, perseverance and time into it.

GOD, I want to surrender myself to You in prayer
by putting enthusiasm, perseverance and time
into it. Amen.

Apostolic Praying

Night and day we pray most earnestly.

1 Thessalonians 3:10

The New Testament preachers laid themselves out in prayer for God's people. They put God in full force into churches by their praying.

The preacher who has never learned in the school of Christ the high and divine art of intercession for his people, will never learn the art of preaching. Though he may be the most gifted genius in sermon making and sermon delivery, he will never preach as the apostles, if he does not pray as they did.

Apostolic praying makes apostolic saints, and keeps apostolic times of purity and power in the church.

DEAR LORD GOD, I want to pray night and day as Your apostles did. Please help me. Amen.

A Spiritual Energy

He has given us His very
great and precious promises.

2 Peter 1:4

Without God's promise, prayer is eccentric and without foundation. It is prayer that makes the promises precious and practical.

Prayer as spiritual energy makes way for, and brings into practical realization, the promises of God.

God's promises cover all things that pertain to life and godliness and that have to do with time and eternity.

These promises bless the present and extend to the eternal future. Promises are God's golden fruit, to be plucked by the hand of prayer.

FATHER, I hold on to Your promises as I pray, so that I may pluck Your golden fruit of grace. Amen.

Humility that Energizes Prayer

My heart is not proud, Lord, my eyes
are not haughty; I do not concern myself with
great matters or things too wonderful for me.

Psalm 131:1

Humility holds in its keeping the very life of prayer. Neither pride nor vanity can pray. It is a positive quality, a substantial force that energizes prayer. There is no power in prayer to ascend without it.

Humility springs from a lowly estimate of ourselves and of our deserving. To be clothed with humility is to be clothed with a praying garment.

Humility is realizing our unworthiness, the feeling and declaring of ourselves as sinners because we are sinners. Kneeling suits us very well as the physical posture of prayer because it speaks of humility.

ALMIGHTY GOD, I confess that I'm a sinner. Please forgive my sins and clothe me with a praying garment of humility. Amen.

Promising Prayer

Be joyful in hope, patient in affliction,
faithful in prayer.

Romans 12:12

Prayer and God's promises are interdependent. The promise inspires and energizes prayer, but prayer locates the promise and gives it realization and location.

The promise is like the blessed rain falling in full showers. But prayer, like the pipes that direct the rain, focus these promises until they become direct and personal – until they bless, refresh, and fertilize.

Prayer takes hold of the promise and guides it to its marvelous end, removes the obstacles, and makes a highway for the promise to reach its glorious fulfillment.

★ ★ ★

DEAR LORD GOD, thank You that our earnest prayers can put Your promises to bless and refresh in action. I praise Your name. Amen.

Elijah

"Go and present yourself to Ahab,
and I will send rain on the land."

1 Kings 18:1

Many glorious results marked that day of heroic faith and dauntless courage on Elijah's part. The happening on Mount Carmel had been successful, but there was no rain. The one thing, the only thing, that God had promised, had not been given.

Elijah turned from Israel to God and from Baal to the one Source of help for a final victory. But it was only until the seventh time that the promise was fulfilled.

Elijah's relentless praying bore to its triumphant results the promise of God, and rain descended in full showers.

ALMIGHTY GOD, please help me to pray relentlessly like Elijah did, so that Your glorious promises can be fulfilled. Amen.

The Prayer of Submission

You do not have, because you do not ask God.

James 4:2

Our prayers are too little and feeble to execute the purposes of God with appropriating power. Marvelous purposes need marvelous praying to execute them. How great, how sublime, and how exalted are the promises God makes to His people!

Prayer is based on the purpose and promise of God. Prayer is submission to God. Prayer is never disloyal to God. It may cry out in times of trouble, but it is rewarded with God's glory.

★ ★ ★

FATHER, I want my prayers to be based on Your purposes and promises. Please guide me. Amen.

According to God's Will

Being strengthened with all power
according to His glorious might so that you
may have great endurance and patience.

Colossians 1:11

Prayer is conscious conformity to God's will, based upon the direct promise of God's Word, and under the application of the Holy Spirit.

Nothing is surer than that the Word of God is the foundation of prayer. We pray just as we believe God's Word.

Prayer is based directly and specifically upon God's revealed promises in Christ Jesus. It has no other ground upon which to base its plea. Not our feelings, not our merits, not our works, but God's promise is the basis of faith and the solid ground of prayer.

DEAR GOD, I base my prayers on Your revealed promises in Christ Jesus. Your Word is the foundation of my prayers. I praise Your holy name. Amen.

Chained by Prayer

"Therefore I tell you, whatever you
ask for in prayer, believe that you have
received it, and it will be yours."

Mark 11:24

God's promises are dependent on our prayer. The
promises are planted in us, appropriated by us, and
held in the arms of faith by prayer. Prayer gives the
promises their efficiency and utilizes them. Prayer
puts the promises to practical and present uses.

Promises, like the rain, are general. Prayer em-
bodies, precipitates, and locates them for personal
use. The promises, like electricity, may sparkle and
dazzle and yet remain useless for good until these
dynamic, life-giving currents are chained by prayer
and become mighty forces that move and bless.

FATHER GOD, thank You that our prayers can
put Your promises to practical and present uses.
All we have to do is believe in Your mighty name.
Amen.

Answer to Prayer

"Ask ... seek ... knock ... it will be given to
you ... you will find ... the door will be opened to you."

Matthew 7:7

Answered prayer brings praying out of the realm of
dry, dead things and makes praying a thing of life
and power. It is the answer to prayer that brings
things to pass, and orders all things according to the
will of God.

It is the answer to prayer that makes praying real.
It is the answer to prayer that makes praying a power
for God and for man, and makes praying real and
divine.

DEAR LORD, I want to thank You for answering
our prayers. We must only ask and believe. You
will answer in good time. Amen.

Prayer ... without Heart?

Never be lacking in zeal, but keep your
spiritual fervor, serving the Lord.

Romans 12:11

Prayer, without burning enthusiasm does not help your situation, because it has nothing to give.

Prayer without enthusiasm has no heart. Heart, soul and mind must find a place in real praying. Heaven must be moved to feel the force of this crying unto God.

Paul was a notable example of a man with a fervent spirit of prayer. His petitioning was all-consuming. It centered immovably upon the object of his desire and the God who was able to meet it.

★ ★ ★

DEAR GOD, I want to have the fervent spirit of Paul. Please guide me in Your truth today. Amen.

— 31 —

School of Trouble

Who shall separate us from the love of Christ?
Shall trouble or hardship or persecution or
famine or nakedness or danger or sword?

Romans 8:35

What an infinite variety there is in the troubles of
life! No two people have the same troubles in a
certain area. God deals with no two of His children
in the same way.

Just as God varies His treatment of His children,
so trouble is varied. God does not repeat Himself; He
does not have one pattern that He uses for everyone.
He deals with every child individually, according to
his or her specific situation.

LORD, troubles come in various shapes and
sizes. Thank You for treating each of Your children
in a unique and special way. Amen.

Feeble Prayer

Then Jesus told His disciples a parable
to show them that they should always
pray and not give up.

Luke 18:1

Our Lord warns us against feeble prayer. This means that we must possess enough enthusiasm to carry us through the severe and long periods of pleading prayer. Fire makes one alert, vigilant, and brings one out as more than a conqueror.

The atmosphere about us is too heavily charged with resisting forces for lifeless prayers to make any progress. It takes heat, fervency and fire to push through to the heavens where God dwells with His saints.

Fervency before God counts in the hour of prayer and finds a speedy and rich reward at God's hands.

DEAR FATHER, please grant me heat, fervency and fire to push through my troubles and toward You in heaven. Amen.

Trouble Has No Power

"He causes His sun to rise on the
evil and the good, and sends rain on
the righteous and the unrighteous."

Matthew 5:45

As trouble is not sinful in itself, neither is it the evidence of sin. Good and bad alike experience trouble. Trouble is no evidence whatsoever of divine displeasure. Numerous Scripture verses contradict such an idea.

Job is an example of where God bore explicit testimony to his deep piety, and yet permitted Satan to afflict Job beyond any other man for wise and beneficial purposes. Trouble has no power in itself to interfere with the relationship of a saint to God.

DEAR GOD, I know that trouble has no power to interfere with my relationship with You. For that, I thank You. Amen.

A Fervent Spirit

As the deer pants for streams of water,
so my soul pants for You, my God.
My soul thirsts for God, for the living God.
When can I go and meet with God?

Psalm 42:1-2

Fervency has its seat in the heart, not in the brain or intellect of the mind. Fervency is the pulse and movement of the emotional nature.

It is not our job to create fervency of spirit at our own command, but we can ask God to plant it in our hearts. Then, it is ours to nourish and cherish.

The process of personal salvation is not just to pray and express our desires to God, but to acquire a fervent spirit and seek to cultivate it.

Ask God to create a spirit of fervent prayer in you and keep it alive.

FATHER, I pray that You will plant in me fervency of spirit. I also ask You to help and guide me in nourishing and cherishing this fervency of heart. Amen.

When Trouble Comes

"Come to Me, all you who are weary
and burdened, and I will give you rest."

Matthew 11:28

The most natural thing to do is to carry your troubles to the Lord and seek grace, patience and submission there. How natural and reasonable for the oppressed, broken, bruised soul to bow low and seek the face of God!

Unfortunately, trouble does not always drive people to God in prayer. It is sad when a person does not know how to pray when troubles discourage him. Blessed is the man who is driven by trouble to his knees in prayer!

★　★　★

ALMIGHTY GOD, I carry all my worries and burdens to You. I know that You will comfort me and give me rest. Thank You. Amen.

The Objective of Desire

The eyes of the LORD range throughout the earth to strengthen those whose hearts are fully committed to Him. You have done a foolish thing, and from now on you will be at war.

2 Chronicles 16:9

Fervency, just like prayer, has to do with God. Desire always has an objective. If we desire at all, we desire *something*. The degree of enthusiasm with which we form our spiritual desires will always serve to determine the earnestness of our praying.

Prayer must be clothed with fervency, strength, and power. It is the force that, centered on God, determines the amount of Himself given out for earthly good.

People who are fervent in spirit are bent on attaining righteousness, and all the other characteristics that God desires His children to have.

DEAR GOD, clothe me with fervency, strength and power through Your indwelling Spirit. In Jesus' name I pray. Amen.

Trouble and Prayer

No temptation has seized you
except what is common to man.

1 Corinthians 10:13

Trouble and prayer are closely related to each other. Prayer is of great value to trouble. Trouble often drives people to God in prayer, while prayer is but the voice of people in trouble. There is great value in prayer in times of trouble.

Prayer often delivers one from trouble and, more often, gives strength to bear trouble, ministers comfort in trouble, and creates patience in the midst of trouble.

Wise is the person who knows his True Source of strength and who doesn't fail to pray in times of trouble.

GOD, thank You, for delivering me in times of trouble. I know that there is power and great value in prayer. I praise Your name. Amen.

Not Just Sunshine and Pleasure

Man born of woman
is of few days and full of trouble.

Job 14:1

Trouble is part of a person's everyday life on earth. Trouble has the power to fill a person with unnecessary despair and stress.

The view of life that expects nothing but sunshine and looks only for pleasure and flowers, is an entirely false view and shows supreme ignorance. It is such people who are so sadly disappointed and surprised when trouble breaks into their lives.

These are the people who don't know God, who know nothing of His disciplinary dealings with His people and who are prayerless.

GOD, You say in Your Word that we will never be tempted beyond what we can bear. Thank You for delivering us in times of trouble when we come to You in prayer. Amen.

All My Longings ...

All my longings lie open before You, LORD;
my sighing is not hidden from You.

Psalm 38:9

What a cheerful thought! Our groanings are not hidden from the eyes of the Lord to whom we pray.

The incentive for fervency of spirit before God is exactly the same as it is for consistent prayer. While fervency is not prayer, it flows from an earnest soul and is precious in the sight of God. Fervency in prayer is the forerunner of what God will do in answer to prayer.

When we seek His face in prayer, God has to give us the desires of our hearts in proportion to the fervency of spirit we exhibit.

DEAR FATHER, I seek Your face as I come to You in prayer. I pray for my fervency of spirit to increase. Amen.

Trouble as God's Servant

In this you greatly rejoice, though now for a little while you may have had to suffer grief in all kinds of trials. These have come so that your faith may be proved genuine and may result in praise, glory and honor when Jesus Christ is revealed.

1 Peter 1:6-7

Trouble is under the control of God and is one of His most efficient agents in fulfilling His purposes and in perfecting His saints. God's hand is in every trouble that happens in the lives of His people.

This is not to say that He directly and randomly orders every unpleasant experience of life or that He is personally responsible for every painful and afflicting thing. However, no trouble is ever turned loose in this world, but it comes with divine permission to do its painful work with God's hand involved, carrying out His gracious acts of redemption.

★ ★ ★

O LORD, You are involved in every aspect of my life. Thank You for being near me in times of trouble. Amen.

Red Hot Prayer

John answered them all, "I baptize you
with water. But one more powerful than
I will come, the thongs of whose sandals
I am not worthy to untie. He will baptize
you with the Holy Spirit and with fire."

Luke 3:16

Prayers must be red hot. It is the fervent prayer that is effective. It takes fire to make prayers work. God wants warmhearted servants. We are to be baptized with the Holy Spirit and with fire.

Fervency is warmth of soul. If our faith does not set us on fire, it is because our hearts have become cold. God dwells in a flame; the Holy Spirit descends in fire. To be absorbed in God's will and to be so earnest about doing His will, is a symptom of a believer who prays effectively.

DEAR GOD, You promised in Your Word that You would give us a new heart and a new spirit. I want my prayers to You to have power and bring change. Amen.

— **42** —

Under Divine Control

We know that in all things God works
for the good of those who love Him.

Romans 8:28

This Scripture verse is so often quoted, but the depth of its meaning is rarely fully grasped. All things are under God's divine control. Trouble is neither above nor beyond His control. It is not independent of God at all.

No matter from what source trouble springs or from where it arises, God is sufficiently wise and able to lay His hand upon it and work it into His plans and purposes concerning the highest welfare of His people.

★   ★   ★

FATHER GOD, I know that all things work together for the good of those who love You. Thank You for having my highest welfare in Your plans. Amen.

A Season of Trial

The Lord disciplines those He loves, and
He punishes everyone He accepts as a son.

Hebrews 12:6

Trouble belongs to the disciplinary part of the government of God. This is a life where the human race is on probation. It is a season of trial.

Trouble does not always arise to punish a person. It belongs to what the Scriptures call "chastening". Strictly speaking, punishment does not belong to this life. God wants to discipline His people. Disciplining is corrective processes in His plans concerning man.

It is because of this that prayer comes in when trouble arises. Prayer should be part of every aspect of your day-to-day life!

O FATHER, help me to see that disciplining from You is a corrective process in Your plans concerning me. Amen.

Divine Discipline

Consider it pure joy, my brothers, whenever
you face trials of many kinds, because you know
that the testing of your faith develops perseverance.

James 1:2-3

Three words are used in the descriptions of divine discipline: temptation, trial and trouble. Temptation is really evil arising from the Devil or born in the nature of man.

Trial is testing. It proves us, tests us, and makes us stronger when we submit to the trial and work together with God to overcome it.

The third word is trouble, which covers all the painful, grievous events of life.

It is enough to know that trouble in God's hand becomes His agent to accomplish His gracious work concerning those who recognize Him in prayer, and who work together with Him.

GOD, thank You, that You use trouble in our lives
to accomplish Your gracious work. Amen.

Divine Providence

For hardship does not spring from the soil,
nor does trouble sprout from the ground. Yet man
is born to trouble as surely as sparks fly upward.

Job 5:6-7

Let us accept the idea that trouble does not arise by chance, nor does it occur by accident. Trouble naturally belongs to God's moral government and is one of His invaluable agents in governing the world.

When we realize this, we can better understand much of what is recorded in the Scriptures and can have a clearer concept of God's dealings with ancient Israel.

In God's dealings with them, we find what is called a history of Divine Providence.

★   ★   ★

ALMIGHTY GOD, I realize that You can use our troubles to accomplish great things in this world for Your glory. Thank You, Lord. Amen.

The Most
Appropriate Thing

"Call on Me in the day of trouble;
I will deliver you, and you will honor Me."

Psalm 50:15

There is a distinct note of comfort in John's gospel for the praying saints of the Lord. Jesus Himself said to His disciples, "I will not leave you as orphans" (John 14:18). All this has been said so that we may realize the necessity of prayer in trouble.

In times of trouble, where does prayer come in? Prayer is the most appropriate thing for a soul to do in times of trouble. Prayer recognizes God in the day of trouble.

Prayer sees God's hand in the midst of trouble and prays to Him. Blessed is he who knows how to turn to God in times of trouble.

GOD, when the troubles of life have left me destitute, please help me to turn to You in prayer, for You will deliver me. Amen.

Prayer Brings Comfort

It was good for me to be afflicted
so that I might learn Your decrees.

Psalm 119:71

Prayer in times of trouble brings comfort, help, hope and blessings that, while not making the trouble disappear, enable the saint to handle it better and to submit to the will of God.

Prayer opens the eyes to see God's hand in trouble. Prayer does not interpret God's providence, but it does justify it and recognize God in it. Prayer enables us to see wise ends in trouble. Prayer in trouble drives us away from unbelief, saves us from doubt, and delivers us from all vain and foolish questioning because of our painful experiences.

FATHER, please help me to pray in trouble so that I can be saved from doubt through Your mercy and grace. Amen.

All Kinds of Troubles

"Each day has enough trouble of its own."

Matthew 6:34

Some troubles only exist in the mind. Some are anticipated troubles that never come. Others are past troubles, and it is foolish to worry over them. Present troubles are the only ones requiring attention and demanding prayer.

Some troubles are self-originated; we are their authors. Some of these originate involuntarily; some arise from our ignorance; some come from our carelessness.

All this can be readily admitted without breaking the force of the statement that troubles are the subjects of prayer and should therefore drive us to prayer.

ALMIGHTY GOD, I pray that You will open my eyes in my times of trouble to realize that I only need to come to You in prayer. Amen.

In All Things

For our light and momentary troubles are achieving
for us an eternal glory that far outweighs them all.

2 Corinthians 4:17

Some troubles are human in their origin. They arise
from secondary causes. They originate with other
people, but we are the sufferers. Who has not at
some time suffered at the hands of others? But even
these are allowed to happen in the order of God's
providence, and may be prayed over.

Why should we not carry our hurts, our wrongs,
and our hardships, caused by the acts of others to
God in prayer? Are such things outside the realm of
prayer? Are they exceptions to the rule of prayer?
Not at all. God can and will lay His hand upon all
such events in answer to prayer.

FATHER GOD, I bring all my hurts, wrongs and
hardships to You in prayer. Thank You for laying
Your hand upon my life to heal my suffering.
Amen.

To See God in All

The LORD gave and the LORD has taken away;
may the name of the LORD be praised.

Job 1:21

When we survey all the sources from which trouble comes, we realize two invaluable truths: first, our troubles, in the end, are of the Lord. He is in all of them and is interested in us when they press and bruise us.

Secondly, in our troubles, no matter what the cause, whether of ourselves or people or devils or even God Himself, we are warranted in taking them to God in prayer and seeking to get the greatest spiritual benefits out of them.

DEAR GOD, I want to see Your face and praise Your name even in the midst of my troubles. Please guide me through Your Holy Spirit. Amen.

Prayer Prepares the Heart

This poor man called, and the LORD
heard him; He saved him out of all his troubles.

Psalm 34:6

Prayer in times of trouble tends to bring the spirit into perfect submission to the will of God, and delivers from everything like a rebellious heart or a critical spirit. Prayer sanctifies trouble to our highest good.

Prayer so prepares the heart that it softens under the disciplining hand of God.

Prayer allows God to freely work with us and in us in the day of trouble. Prayer lifts our burdens and brings to us the sweetest, the highest and greatest good.

Prayer permits God's servant – trouble – to accomplish its mission in us, with us, and for us.

DEAR FATHER, help me to see that my prayers allow You to work freely with me and in me in the day of trouble. Amen.

A Positive Spirit

"Because he loves Me," says the LORD,
"I will rescue him; I will protect him,
for he acknowledges My name. He will call
upon Me, and I will answer him; I will be with
him in trouble, I will deliver him and honor him."

Psalm 91:14-15

The end of trouble is always good in the mind of God. If trouble fails in its mission, it is either because of a lack of prayer or unbelief, or both. The good or evil of trouble is always determined by the spirit in which it is received.

Trouble proves a blessing or a curse, depending on how it is received and treated by us. It either softens or hardens us. It either draws us to prayer and to God or drives us away.

The sun can either soften the wax or harden the clay. The sun can either melt the ice or dry out moisture from the earth.

DEAR GOD, please grant me a positive spirit so that I will see the end of trouble as good. Amen.

God's Promises

"Test Me in this" says the Lᴏʀᴅ Almighty.

Malachi 3:10

God's great promises find their fulfillment along the lines of prayer.

In this connection, let it be noted that God's promises are always personal and specific. They deal with people. Each believer can claim the promise as his own. God deals with each one personally, so that every person can put the promises to the test.

The praying saint has the right to put his hand upon God's promises and claim them as his own, made especially for him and intended to embrace all his needs, both present and future.

GOD ALMIGHTY, I claim Your promises in Your Word as my own today. Thank You that You always keep Your promises. Amen.

The Promised Messiah

"Your prayer has been heard."

Luke 1:13

God had promised through His prophets that the coming Messiah would have a forerunner. How many homes and wombs in Israel had longed for this great honor?

Perhaps Zechariah and Elizabeth were the only ones who realized this great dignity and blessing by praying for it.

It was then that the Word of the Lord, as spoken by the prophets, and the prayers of Zechariah and his wife brought John the Baptist into the withered womb and into the childless home of Zechariah and Elizabeth.

THANK YOU, dear Father, for always keeping Your promises. Amen.

Make the Promise Real!

I urge you, brothers, by our Lord Jesus Christ
and by the love of the Spirit, to join me
in my struggle by praying to God for me.

Romans 15:30

How did Paul make this promise efficient? How did he make the promise real? Here is the answer. Paul asked his brothers in Christ to pray for him.

Their prayers, united with his prayer, were to secure his deliverance and secure his safety, and were also to make the apostolic promise vital and cause it to be fully realized.

All is to be sanctified and realized by the Word of God and prayer. God's deep and wide river of promise will be life-giving waters to our hearts.

 ★ ★ ★

FATHER, You want us to unite with other believers to make Your promises real and efficient. Guide me in requesting my fellow believers to pray for me. Amen.

Give Your All

"In that day you will no longer ask Me anything.
I tell you the truth, My Father will give you
whatever you ask in My name. Ask and you
will receive, and your joy will be complete."

John 16:23-24

God has committed Himself to us by His Word through our prayers. The Word of God is the basis, the inspiration, and the heart of prayer.

Jesus Christ stands as the illustration of God's Word and its unlimited goodness in promise as well as in realization. God takes nothing by halves. He gives nothing by halves. We can have the whole of Him when He has the whole of us.

These often-heard promises seem to daze us, and instead of allowing them to move us to asking and receiving, we turn away full of wonder, but empty-handed and with empty hearts.

DEAR GOD, You commit the whole of Yourself to us. You give nothing by halves. I want to give my all to You. Amen.

Specific Answers to Prayers

"Call to Me and I will answer you."

Jeremiah 33:3

God the Father and Jesus Christ, His Son, are both strongly committed by the truth of the Word and by the integrity of their character to answer prayer.

Not only does this and all the promises pledge God to answer prayer, but they assure us that the answer will be specific.

Our Lord's invariable teaching was that we will receive whatever we ask for in prayer. If we ask for bread, He will give us bread. If we ask for an egg, He will give us an egg. Evil will not be given to us in answer to prayer, rather God's goodness.

ALMIGHTY GOD, thank You for answering our prayers specifically like we request. Amen.

A Compassionate Savior

We have one who has been tempted in
every way, just as we are – yet was without sin.

Hebrews 4:15

Jesus Christ was altogether man. He was the divine
Son of God, yet at the same time He was the human
Son of God.

This allowed our Lord to be a compassionate
Savior. It is no sin to feel the pain and realize the
darkness on the path into which God leads us.
It is only human to cry out against the pain and
desolation of the hour.

How strong it makes us to have one True North
to guide us to the glory of God!

★   ★   ★

LORD GOD, thank You that because You have
been tempted in every way while on earth, You
understand our struggles perfectly. I look to You
as my guiding light. Amen.

Our Heavenly Father

"If you, then, though you are evil, know
how to give good gifts to your children,
how much more will your Father in heaven
give good gifts to those who ask Him!"

Matthew 7:11

Earthly parents give when asked and respond to the crying of their children. The encouragement to pray is transferred from our earthly father to our heavenly Father – from the weak to the omnipotent. Our heavenly Father is the highest conception of fatherhood.

He will supply all our needs, more than our earthly fathers can, and He will enable us to meet every difficult duty and fulfill every law. Though it may be hard for our flesh and blood to do, it is made easy under the full supply of our Father's divine and everlasting help.

★　★　★

DEAR FATHER GOD, You are the perfect and divine example of fatherhood. I thank You for supplying all my needs. Amen.

God Cannot Lie

A faith and knowledge resting on the hope
of eternal life, which God, who does not lie,
promised before the beginning of time.

Titus 1:2

God explicitly says: There are no limitations, no
hedges, no hindrances in the way of Me fulfilling My
promises. Man is to look for the answer, be inspired
by the expectation of the answer, and demand the
answer with humble boldness.

God, who cannot lie, is bound to answer. The
people of God in biblical times were unshaken in
their faith in the absolute certainty that God would
fulfill His promises to them. They rested in security
on the Word of God.

Thus, their history is marked by repeated asking
and receiving at the hands of God.

SOVEREIGN GOD, I know that there are no
hindrances, limitations or hedges in You fulfilling
Your promises. You are Truth. I praise Your name.
Amen.

Prayer That Motivates God

*"Suppose one of you has a friend, and he
goes to him at midnight and says, 'Friend,
lend me three loaves of bread.'"*

Luke 11:5-6

The purpose of Christ's teachings is to declare that
His followers are to pray earnestly.

All these qualities of the soul are brought out
in the parable of the man who went to his friend
for bread at midnight. This man did his task with
confidence. He could not go back empty-handed.
The flat refusal shamed and surprised him. Here even
friendship failed! But there was still something to be
tried – stern resolution and fixed determination.

He would stay and pursue his demand until the
door was opened. He proceeded to do this and, by
persistence, secured what ordinary requesting had
failed to obtain.

DEAR FATHER, thank You for teaching us
through Your Word that persistence in prayer
yields results. Amen.

An Act of Holiness

Make every effort to live in peace
with all men and to be holy; without
holiness no one will see the Lord.

Hebrews 12:14

Unfortunately, we have substituted the external for the internal. Even in the church, we are much further advanced in material matters than in spiritual matters.

It is largely due to the decline of prayer. With the decline of the work of holiness has come the decline of the business of praying. We may excuse it, yet it is all too clear that the emphasis in the work of the present-day church is not on prayer.

The church is not producing praying men and women, because the church is not intently engaged in this one great work of holiness.

DEAR GOD, I pray that our church will engage again in the act of holiness. I pray that our church will produce praying men and women for Your glory. Amen.

Forceless Prayers

Those who know Your name will
trust in You, for You, LORD, have
never forsaken those who seek You.

Psalm 9:10

Persistent prayer is the earnest, inward movement of the heart toward God. Isaiah lamented that no one stirred himself to take hold of God. There was much praying done in Isaiah's time, but it was indifferent and self-righteous.

There were no mighty moves of souls toward God. There was no array of sanctified energies bent on reaching God. There was no energy to draw the treasures of His grace from Him.

Forceless prayers have no power to overcome difficulties, get results, or gain complete victories. We must win God before we can win our plea.

DEAR LORD GOD, I want my prayers to
be forceful. I want my prayers to be an inward
movement of my heart toward You so that You
will be glorified by them. Amen.

Persistent Prayer

In the last days the mountain of the
LORD's temple will be established as chief
among the mountains; it will be raised above
the hills, and all nations will stream to it.

Isaiah 2:2

Isaiah looked with hopeful eyes to the day when faith would flourish and there would be times of real praying. Times in which our prayers would keep all spiritual interests busy and make increasing demands on God's exhaustless treasures.

Persistent prayer never hesitates or grows weary. It is never discouraged. It never yields to cowardice, but is lifted up and sustained by a hope that knows no despair and a faith that will not let go.

Persistent prayer has patience to wait and strength to continue. It never prepares itself to quit praying, and it refuses to get up from its knees until an answer is received.

ALMIGHTY GOD, Keep me on my knees, until my prayers are answered. Thank You, Lord. Amen.

Ask, Seek and Knock

"Ask and it will be given to you; seek and you
will find; knock and the door will be opened to you."

Matthew 7:7

These are the ringing challenges of our Lord regarding
prayer. These challenges are His explanation that
true praying must wait and advance in effort and
urgency until the prayer is answered.

In the three words *ask, seek* and *knock*, Jesus, by
the order in which He places them, urges the necessity of persistence in prayer. Asking, seeking,
and knocking are ascending rungs in the ladder of
successful prayer.

No principle is more definitely enforced by
Christ than that successful prayer must contain the
qualities of waiting and persevering.

FATHER GOD, I want the qualities that waits
and perseveres to be in my prayers. Please guide
me as I ask, seek and knock when I pray. Amen.

Keep on Praying

As Jesus went on from there,
two blind men followed Him, calling out,
"Have mercy on us, Son of David!"

Matthew 9:27

The most important qualities in Christ's estimate of the highest form of praying are unbeatable courage and stability of purpose.

Even if God does not answer our prayers right away, we must keep on praying. In Matthew we have the first record of the miracle of healing the blind. We have an illustration of how our Lord did not seem to hear immediately those who sought Him. But the two blind men continued with their petitions. He did not answer them and went into the house.

The needy ones followed Him and, finally, gained their eyesight and their plea.

ALMIGHTY GOD, I pray for courage and stability of purpose to persevere until my prayers are answered. Amen.

The Case of the Blind Bartimaeus

When he heard that it was
Jesus of Nazareth, he began to shout,
"Jesus, Son of David, have mercy on me!"

Mark 10:47

The case of the blind Bartimaeus is noteworthy in many ways.

At first, Jesus seemed not to hear. The crowd rebuked the noisy babbling of Bartimaeus. Despite the apparent unconcern of our Lord and the rebuke of an impatient crowd, the blind beggar still cried out. He increased the loudness of his cry until Jesus was moved.

Finally, the crowd, as well as Jesus, listened and spoke in favor of his cause. He won his case. His persistence won where half-hearted indifference would surely have failed.

DEAR LORD, have mercy on me, a sinner. I ask this in Jesus' name. Amen.

Persistence's Importance

On reaching the place, He said to them,
"Pray that you will not fall into temptation."

Luke 22:40

Faith functions in connection with prayer and persistence. Persistence cultivates the belief that prayer will be answered. A person with a persistent spirit will be blessed.

The absolute necessity of persistent prayer is plainly stated in the Word of God and needs to be restated today. Love of ease, spiritual laziness, and religious indifference all operate against this type of petitioning.

Our praying, however, needs to be coaxed with an energy that never tires. It needs to have a persistency that will not be denied and a courage that never fails.

★　★　★

DEAR LORD GOD, inspire my praying with an energy that never tires so that I can come to the place where my faith takes hold of Your blessings. Amen.

A Season of Prayer

Moses sought the favor of the Lord his God.
"O Lord," he said, "why should Your anger burn
against Your people, whom You brought out of
Egypt with great power and a mighty hand?"

Exodus 32:11

Moses furnished us with an excellent example of persistence in prayer. Instead of allowing his intimacy with God to release him from the necessity for persistence, he regarded it as an important aspect of prayer.

When Israel set up the golden calf, the wrath of God increased fiercely against them. Jehovah, bent on executing justice, told Moses what He intended to do. But Moses would not accept the verdict. He threw himself down before the Lord in an agony of intercession on behalf of the sinning Israelites.

For forty days and forty nights he fasted and prayed. What a season of persistent prayer that was!

DEAR FATHER, thank You for Moses' example of what it means to pray persistently. Amen.

Delays and Denials

We, who with unveiled faces all reflect
the Lord's glory, are being transformed
into His likeness with ever-increasing glory,
which comes from the Lord, who is the Spirit.

2 Corinthians 3:18

We need to give thought to the mysterious fact of prayer – the certainty that there will be delays and denials. We must prepare for and permit these delays and denials. The praying Christian is like a brave soldier who, as the conflict grows more severe, exhibits more courage. When delay and denial come, he increases his earnest asking and does not stop until prayer prevails.

There can be no question about persistent prayer moving God and improving human character. If we were more in agreement with God in the command of intercession, our faces would shine more brightly.

GOD, help me to wait patiently for Your answers to my prayers. I know that through making me wait You strengthen my character. Amen.

What Is God's Work in This World?

The reason the Son of God appeared
was to destroy the devil's work.

1 John 3:8

God has a great task on hand in this world. This task is involved in the plan of salvation. It embraces redemption and providence.

What, then, is God's work in this world? God's work is to make the hearts and lives of His children holy. Man is a fallen creature, born with an evil nature. God's entire plan is to take hold of fallen man and to seek to change him and make him holy.

God's work is to make holy soldiers out of unholy people. This is the very reason Christ came into the world.

DEAR FATHER, take hold of me, a fallen person. Change me, and make me holy. Amen.

Be Holy

Just as He who called you is holy,
so be holy in all you do; for it is written:
"Be holy, because I am holy."

1 Peter 1:15-16

God is holy in nature and in all His ways, and He wants to make man like Himself. He wants man to be Christlike. This is the aim of all Christian effort. We must therefore constantly and earnestly pray to be made holy.

Not that we are to *do* holy, but rather to *be* holy. Being must precede doing. First be, then do. First obtain a holy heart, then live a holy life. And for this high and gracious end, God has made the most ample provisions in the atoning work of our Lord and through the agency of the Holy Spirit.

DEAR GOD, I want to be more like You every day. I want to be holy like You are holy. Make my heart holy so that I can live a life pleasing to You. Amen.

Praying Is not Child's Play

During the days of Jesus' life on earth, He offered up
prayers and petitions with loud cries and tears to the
one who could save Him from death, and He was
heard because of His reverent submission.

Hebrews 5:7

Praying is no light and trivial exercise. It engages all
the powers of man's moral and spiritual nature as
is evident in the Scripture verse above about the
praying of our Lord.

It takes only a moment's thought to see how
such praying drew mightily upon all the powers of
God and called into effect every part of His nature.
This is the kind of praying that brings the soul close
to God and that brings God down to earth.

While children should be taught to pray early
on, praying is no child's task. Prayer draws upon the
whole nature of man – body, soul and spirit.

★ ★ ★

DEAR LORD, thank You for Your example of
what it really means to pray. Amen.

Business Integrity

The LORD detests men of perverse heart but
He delights in those whose ways are blameless.

Proverbs 11:20

Again let us ask: Are our leading laymen examples of holiness? Does business integrity and honesty run parallel with religious activity and Christian observance?

If God's work is to make men and women holy – and He has made ample provisions in the law of doing this very thing – why should it be thought impertinent and useless to express such personal and pointed questions such as these?

They deal directly with the work of God and with its progress and its perfection. These questions go to the very center of the disease. They hit the spot.

DEAR GOD, You chose me to be holy and
blameless in Your sight, even before Creation.
Please help me, Lord, to live a life pleasing to You.
Amen.

Material vs. Spiritual Prosperity

"For where your treasure is,
there your heart will be also."

Matthew 6:21

Material prosperity is not a sign of spiritual prosperity. It may blind the eyes of church leaders, so much so that they will make it a substitute for spiritual prosperity. We must be careful not to do this.

Financial prosperity does not signify growth in holiness. The seasons of material prosperity are rarely seasons of spiritual advance, either to the individual or to the church. It is so easy to lose sight of God when wealth increases. It is so easy to lean on human agencies and cease praying and relying upon God when material prosperity comes to the church.

Focus your eyes on God to ensure that your spirit will grow in holiness.

★　★　★

O GOD, I pray that my spirit will grow and prosper in holiness. Amen.

Outpouring of the Holy Spirit

Surely the arm of the LORD is not too
short to save, nor His ear too dull to hear.

Isaiah 59:1

If the work of God is progressing and we are growing in holiness, then some perplexing questions arise. If the church is making advances on the lines of deep spirituality – if we are praying people, and if our people are hungering after holiness, why do we have so few mighty outpourings of the Holy Spirit?

There is only one answer for this state of things. We have cultivated other things, to the neglect of the work of holiness. We have permitted our minds to be preoccupied with material things in the church. We need to focus our eyes on the Lord so that He can pour His Spirit out on us.

ALMIGHTY GOD, I keep myself occupied with unimportant matters instead of focusing on You. Guide me in Your truth today. Amen.

The Work of God

> He will be an instrument for noble
> purposes, made holy, useful to the Master
> and prepared to do any good work.
>
> *2 Timothy 2:21*

People who dedicate themselves to the work of God must focus on the giving and receiving of grace and not on the receiving of gifts. A full supply of grace brings an increase of gifts.

It may be repeated that no results, a low experience, and pointless, powerless preaching always flow from a lack of grace. And a lack of grace flows from a lack of praying.

Great grace comes from great praying. In carrying out His great work in the world, God works through human agents. He works through His church collectively and through His people individually.

DEAR GOD, make me a holy instrument for Your noble purposes. Make me useful and prepare me to do any good work for Your glory. Amen.

Recognized by our Fruit

"Thus, by their fruit you will recognize them."

Matthew 7:20

The world judges religion not by what the Bible says, but by how Christians live. Christians are the Bible that sinners read. The emphasis, then, is placed on holiness of life. In selecting church workers, the quality of holiness is not considered.

Prayer may seem insignificant in the eyes of the world, but it is important in all of God's movements and in all of His plans. He looks for holy people, those noted for their praying habits. As a child of God, bear fruit in such a way that the world may see to whom you belong.

Ask the Spirit of God to guide you to a more holy life.

FATHER GOD, I want to bear good fruit so that the world can see to whom I belong. Guide me to a more holy life. In Jesus' name. Amen.

Spiritual Quality

Do not be deceived: God cannot be mocked.
A man reaps what he sows.

Galatians 6:7

We might wonder why so little is accomplished in the world for the great work that God has in hand. The fact is that it is surprising that so much has been done through people with such weak faith.

Let it be said again and again that holiness of life is the divine standard of religion. Nothing short of this will satisfy the divine requirement. People can do many good things and yet not be holy in heart and righteous in conduct.

Strive towards higher spiritual quality and holiness through Christ Jesus, so that He can use you to do His great work on earth.

O LORD, I want You to use me to do great things for You. I want my actions and my heart to speak of righteousness before You. Please guide me. Amen.

Keep Praying

Then Jesus told His disciples
a parable to show them that they
should always pray and not give up.

Luke 18:1

The success of the persistent man in the face of a flat denial (Luke 11:5-8), was used by the Savior to illustrate the need for perseverance in humble prayer before the throne of heavenly grace.

When the answer is not immediately given, the praying Christian must gather courage at each delay. He must urgently go forward until the answer comes. The answer is assured, if he has the faith to press his petition with vigorous faith.

Negligence, impatience, and fear will be fatal to our prayers. The Father's heart, hand and infinite willingness to hear and give to His children is waiting for the start of our perseverance.

LORD GOD, Strengthen my faith, so that I will gather courage to press on toward a more holy life. Amen.

Whole-Hearted Prayer

May God Himself, the God of peace,
sanctify you through and through. May your
whole spirit, soul and body be kept blameless
at the coming of our Lord Jesus Christ.

1 Thessalonians 5:23

The people of olden times who were very successful
in prayer, who made big things happen, who moved
God to do great things, were those who surrendered
completely to God in their praying.

God requires complete devotion when we pray.
He requires whole-hearted people through whom
He can work out His purposes and plans concerning
all people.

No person with a divided allegiance to God, the
world, and self, can do the praying that is needed.

 ★   ★   ★

DEAR GOD, I surrender my life completely to
You today. I want to give all that I have to You in
prayer. Amen.

The Machinery of Religion

So what shall I do? I will pray with my spirit,
but I will also pray with my mind; I will sing
with my spirit, but I will also sing with my mind.

1 Corinthians 14:15

The church works at religion with the order, precision, and force of real machinery. But too often it works with the heartlessness of the machine. We pray without sincerity and we sing without true joy in our hearts.

We have music without the praise of God being in it or near it. We go to church by habit and come home all too gladly when the benediction is pronounced. We say our prayers by rote, and we are not sorry when the *Amen* is uttered.

Devote your whole heart to God and His church, and see the results of machinery inspired by Christ.

 ★ ★ ★

GOD, I don't want to work for You with the heartlessness of machinery. Please inspire my heart in all that I do for Your glory. Amen.

Our Great High Priest

He offered up prayers and
petitions with loud cries and tears.

Hebrews 5:7

Christ Jesus, our Great High Priest, was a gracious Comforter, and an all-powerful Intercessor. The Holy Spirit enters into all our blessed relations of fellowship and authority, and helps with all the tenderness, fullness and efficiency of Christ.

Was Christ the Christ of prayer? Did He seek the silence, the solitude, and the darkness so that He could pray? Does He sit at the right hand of God in heaven to pray for us there? Of course!

Then how truly does the great Comforter, the Holy Spirit, represent Jesus Christ as the Christ of prayer!

★ ★ ★

ALMIGHTY GOD, I want to thank You for giving us a great High Priest, a gracious Comforter and an all-powerful Intercessor. Amen.

Persistence

You know that the testing of your
faith develops perseverance.

James 1:3

Persistence is the pressing of our desires on God
with urgency and perseverance. It is praying with
courage until our cries are heard.

The man who has an intimate relationship with
God appreciates his privilege of approaching God in
prayer.

Prayer that influences God is said to be the out-
pouring of the fervent, effectual righteous man. It is
prayer on fire.

It does not have a feeble, flickering flame or a momentary spark, but shines with a vigorous, steady
glow.

DEAR GOD, I want my prayers to be effectual.
Ignite my spirit with the vigorous, steady glow of
Your presence so that my prayers may bring You
glory. Amen.

Prayer Can Move the World

"In everything ... present your requests to God."

Philippians 4:6

Prayer is a direct address to God. Prayer secures blessings and betters people because it reaches the ear of God.

Prayer affects people by affecting God. Prayer moves people because it moves God to move them. Prayer moves the hand that moves the world.

The utmost possibilities of prayer have rarely been realized. The promises of God are so great to those who truly pray, that when He puts Himself fully into the hands of the praying ones, it almost staggers our faith and leave us amazed.

DEAR LORD GOD, thank You that our prayers secure blessings and make people better because they reach Your ears. Amen.

Time with God

Is any one of you in trouble? He should pray.
Is anyone happy? Let him sing songs of praise.

James 5:13

Our devotional time is not measured by the clock, but time is of the essence. The ability to stay and wait essentially belongs to our fellowship with God.

Haste is often a part of the great business of communion with God. Short devotional time is the ruin of deep piety. Calmness, and strength are never the companions of haste. Short devotional time drains spiritual vigor and the root and bloom of the spiritual life.

Short devotional time is the number one reason for backsliding. It is a sure indication of superficial piety.

FATHER, forgive me, for not always making enough time for You. I want to stay and wait in Your presence so that I can hear Your voice. Amen.

Praying Costs Time

You help us by your prayers.

2 Corinthians 1:11

Spiritual work is taxing work. Praying requires attention and time, which flesh and blood do not enjoy. Few people devote their time to prayer when earthly duty calls.

We sometimes become lax in our praying, and do not realize the peril until the damage has been done. Hasty devotions make weak faith, feeble convictions, and questionable piety.

To be little with God is to be little for God. To cut the praying short makes the whole Christian character short, miserable and careless.

DEAR LORD GOD, help me to not become lax in my prayers. I want to spend more time with You, so that I can do more for You. Amen.

God's Full Flow

Pray for us that the message of the Lord
may spread rapidly and be honored,
just as it was with you. And pray that we might
be delivered from wicked and evil men.

2 Thessalonians 3:1-2

It takes time for the fullness of God to flow into the spirit. Short devotions cut the pipe of God's full flow. It takes time spent in earnest prayer to receive the full revelation of God. Little time and hurry spoil the picture.

More time and early hours devoted to prayer would revive and invigorate many a dead spiritual life. More time and early hours for prayer would result in holy living. A holy life would not be so rare or so difficult if our devotions were not so short and hurried.

GOD, I know that more time spent with You will revive and invigorate my spiritual life. Please help me to set my priorities straight. You are the most important thing in my life. Amen.

Lingering in God's Presence

"Will not God bring about justice for His
chosen ones, who cry out to Him day and night?"

Luke 18:7

A Christly temper would not be such a foreign thing
if our prayer lives were intensified. We are sometimes
miserable because we do not pray enough.

Time spent with God will bring abundance to our
lives. When we are devoted to God in our personal
quiet time, we will be devoted to Him in public.

Hasty prayers are without results. Lingering in
God's presence instructs and wins. We are taught
by it, and the greatest victories are often the results
of great waiting – waiting until words and plans
are exhausted. Silent and patient waiting gains the
crown.

★ ★ ★

FATHER GOD, I want to linger in Your
presence. I want to cry out to You day and night.
Please guide me. Amen.

Prepared Hearts

Finally, brothers, pray for us that the message
of the Lord may spread rapidly and be honored.

2 Thessalonians 3:1

Prayer means the success of the preaching of the
Word. It creates an atmosphere that is favorable for
the Word to accomplish its purpose.

The parable of the sower is a notable study of
preaching, showing its differing effects and des-
cribing the diversity of hearers. The wayside hearers are many. The soil lies unprepared. As a conse-
quence, the devil easily takes away the seed (which
is the Word of God).

If only the hearers would prepare the ground of
their hearts beforehand by prayer and meditation,
much of the current sowing would be fruitful.

DEAR LORD GOD, help us to prepare the
ground better through our prayers, so that
Your Word will take root in people's hearts and
produce a crop. Amen.

Cultivated Hearts

"Therefore consider carefully how you listen."

Luke 8:18

The parable of the sower shows us the different responses of the stony-ground and thorny-ground hearers. Although the Word lodges in their hearts and begins to sprout, all is lost, mainly because there is no cultivation afterwards.

The good-ground hearers are profited by the sowing, simply because their minds have been prepared for the reception of the seed. After hearing, they have cultivated the seed sown in their hearts by the exercise of prayer.

All this emphasizes the conclusion of this striking parable: In order to carefully consider how we hear, we must give ourselves continually to prayer.

DEAR GOD, I want to hear Your Word and understand it, I want Your message to fall on good soil so that it may yield a crop for Your glory. Amen.

Conduct and Character

Be self-controlled and alert. Your enemy
the devil prowls around like a roaring
lion looking for someone to devour.

1 Peter 5:8

It is true that prayer governs conduct, and conduct shapes character. Conduct is what we do. Character is what we are. Conduct is the outward life. Character is the unseen life, hidden within, yet is evidenced by what is seen. Conduct is external, seen from without. Character is internal, operating within.

In the economy of grace, conduct is the offspring of character. Character is the state of the heart and conduct is its outward expression. Prayer is related to all the gifts of grace. Prayer helps to establish character and to shape conduct. And both depend on prayer for their successful continuance.

FATHER, I know that the successful continuance
of how I act and who I am depend on prayer.
Please guide me in Your truth today. Amen.

The True Test

If My people, who are called by My name,
will humble themselves and pray and seek
My face and turn from their wicked ways,
then will I hear from heaven and will forgive
their sin and will heal their land.

2 Chronicles 7:14

There is much talk today of consecration, and many
are considered consecrated people. A lot of these
people; however, do not grasp the true meaning of
this word. The central trouble with all this false consecration is that there is no prayer in it. Here is the
true test of consecration: it is a life of prayer. Unless
prayer is in the forefront, the consecration is faulty,
deceptive, falsely named.

Does he pray? That is the test of every so-called
consecrated person. Is he a person of prayer? No
consecration is worth a thought if it is devoid of
prayer, and primarily a life of prayer.

LORD, I humble myself before You. I pray and
seek Your face. Please hear my cries to You. Amen.

Inward Spiritual Character

[Jesus Christ] who gave Himself for us to redeem us
from all wickedness and to purify for Himself a people
that are His very own, eager to do what is good.

Titus 2:14

There may be a certain degree of moral character
and conduct independent of prayer, but there cannot be any distinctive religious character and Christian conduct without it. Prayer helps where all other
aids fail. We become better people and we live purer
lives through constant prayer.

The very end and purpose of the atoning work
of Christ is to create religious character and practice
Christian conduct.

In Christ's teaching, it is not simply works of
charity and deeds of mercy that He insists upon, but
inward spiritual character. This much is demanded,
and nothing short of it will be enough.

DEAR GOD, You require an inward spiritual
character which is developed by constant prayer.
Amen.

God's Factory on Earth

For it is God who works in you to will
and to act according to His good purpose.

Philippians 2:13

The purpose of prayer is to change the character and conduct of people. In countless instances, change has been brought about by prayer. The church is presumed to be righteous and should be engaged in turning people to righteousness.

The church is God's factory on earth. Its primary duty is to create and foster righteous character. This is its very highest aim. Primarily, its work is not to acquire members or accumulate numbers. Its aim is not to get money or engage in deeds of charity and works of mercy.

Its work is to produce righteousness of character and purity of the outward life.

 ★ ★ ★

ALMIGHTY GOD, guide and direct our church in turning men to righteousness so that Your name may be glorified on earth through our works. Amen.

The Human Side of Holiness

If you fully obey the LORD your God
and carefully follow all His commands
I give you today, the LORD your God will
set you high above all the nations on earth.

Deuteronomy 28:1

Consecration is not all there is to holiness. Many make serious mistakes at this point. Consecration makes us relatively holy. Our lives become more holy when we live closer to God.

Consecration is the human side of holiness. In this sense, it is self-sanctification. But sanctification, or holiness in its truest and highest sense, is divine, the act of the Holy Spirit working in the heart, making it clean, and putting therein a higher degree of the fruit of the Spirit.

LORD GOD, lead me by the help of Your Holy Spirit to fully obey and follow Your commands so that my life can produce the best fruit. Amen.

Products of Prayer

We demolish arguments and every
pretension that sets itself up against the
knowledge of God, and we take captive every
thought to make it obedient to Christ.

2 Corinthians 10:5

A product reflects and partakes of the character of
the manufacturer that makes it. A righteous church
with a righteous purpose makes righteous people.

Prayer produces cleanliness of heart and purity
of life. It can produce nothing else. Unrighteous
behavior is born in the absence of prayer. The two
go hand in hand. Prayer and sinning cannot keep
company with each other. One or the other must
stop. Get people to pray, and they will stop sinning,
because prayer creates a distaste for sinning. It lifts
the entire nature to a reverent contemplation of
high and holy things.

GOD, I want to pray more often. I want to pray
always so that cleanliness and purity of heart will
be evident in my life. Amen.

Praying in Color

You will keep in perfect peace him whose
mind is steadfast, because he trusts in You.

Isaiah 26:3

Prayer is based on character. What we are with God
determines our influence with Him.

It was the inner character, not the outward ap-
pearance of men like Abraham, Job, David, Moses
and others, that had such great influence with God
in the biblical days. Today, it is not so much our
words, but what we really are that counts with God.
Conduct affects character and counts for much in
our praying.

At the same time, character affects conduct to a
far greater extent and has a superior influence over
prayer. Our inner lives gives color to our praying.

DEAR FATHER, who we really are inside is
what matters to You. I pray again today for You
to create a pure heart within me and to renew my
spirit. Amen.

A Life of Personal Holiness

Let us draw near to God with a sincere heart
in full assurance of faith, having our hearts
sprinkled to cleanse us from a guilty conscience
and having our bodies washed with pure water.

Hebrews 10:22

Consecration is much more than a life of so-called service. It is a life of personal holiness. It is that which brings spiritual power into the heart and brightens up the entire inner man. It is a life that always recognizes God, and a life given up to true prayer.

Full consecration is the highest type of Christian life. It is the one thing for which the believer should aim. He should never be satisfied until he is fully, entirely the Lord's by his own consent. His praying naturally and involuntarily leads up to this one act.

DEAR FATHER GOD, I desire to live a life of full consecration to You. This is my aim. Please help and guide me. Amen.

Praying by Your Life

"Be careful or your hearts will be
weighed down with dissipation, drunkenness
and the anxieties of life, and that day will
close on you unexpectedly like a trap."

Luke 21:34

Christian experience often collapses on the rock of conduct. It is the life that counts. Our praying suffers, like other phases of our religious experience, because of bad living. In early times, preachers were ordered to preach by their lives or not preach at all. Christians everywhere ought to be reminded to pray by their lives or not pray at all. The best preaching, even in the pulpit, is that which is strengthened by the preacher living a godly life.

The most effective work done by people in the pews is accompanied by holiness of life. People preach by their lives, not by their words.

LORD, I want to mirror You to the world through my actions, so that others will believe in You without me having to say a word. Amen.

Prayer of Repentance

If anyone is in Christ, he is a new creation;
the old has gone, the new has come!

2 Corinthians 5:17

The prayer of repentance is surely acceptable to God. He delights in hearing the cries of remorseful sinners. But repentance involves not only sorrow for sin, but turning away from wrongdoing and learning to do good. True repentance produces a change in character and behavior.

We have missed the whole purpose of prayer if it fails to shape our character and correct our behavior. Cold, formal praying may exist side by side with bad behavior, but such praying is no praying at all. Our praying advances in power just as much as it rectifies the life. A prayerful life will grow in purity and devotion to God.

★ ★ ★

DEAR GOD, I confess my sins and lay them before You today. Please forgive me and guide me through Your Spirit so that I can turn away from wrong, and do right instead. Amen.

A Brass Door

Therefore confess your sins to each other
and pray for each other so that you may
be healed. The prayer of a righteous
man is powerful and effective.

James 5:16

The character of the inner life is a condition of effective praying. As the life is, so the praying will be.

The prayer of the righteous always achieves much. Indeed, one may go further and say that it is only the prayer of the righteous that achieves anything at all.

The oppression of our lives often breaks the force of our praying and is like a brass door in the face of prayer.

To have your eyes on God's glory and to be possessed by an earnest desire to please Him in all your ways give power to prayer.

FATHER GOD, clean my life from all wrongdoing. I want my life to be pleasing to You. Amen.

The Fruit of Real Prayer

Be wise about what is good,
and innocent about what is evil.

Romans 16:19

Praying must come out of a clean heart. It must be strengthened by a life striving to obey God.

Let us not forget that, while life is a condition of prayer, prayer is also the condition of righteous living. The fruit of real praying is right living. It causes a person to watch his temper, conversation, and conduct. It leads him to walk cautiously and redeem the time. It enables him to act worthy of being a Christian.

It gives him a high incentive to pursue his pilgrimage consistently by shunning every evil way to walk in the light of God.

DEAR LORD GOD, I know that if I want my prayers to be real, I must live right. Help me to be excellent about what is good, and innocent of evil. Amen.

Many Sides of Prayer

His divine power has given us everything we need
for life and godliness through our knowledge of
Him who called us by His own glory and goodness.

2 Peter 1:3

When we study the multi-sidedness of prayer, we may be surprised at the number of things with which it is connected.

Consecration is one of the things to which prayer is closely related. Prayer leads up to and governs consecration. Much goes under the name of consecration that has no consecration in it. Popular consecration is sadly at fault because it has little or no prayer in it.

Consecration that has not resulted from living a life of prayer is not consecration. Prayer is the one prominent thing in a consecrated life.

FATHER, I know that all that I need for a consecrated life is to pray and to know more of You every day. Amen.

Marvelous Change

He saved us, not because of righteous things
we had done, but because of His mercy.

Titus 3:5

The Christian religion deals with people who are lacking spiritual character and who live unholy lives. It aims to change them so that they can become holy in heart and righteous in life.

This is where prayer enters and demonstrates its wonderful ability and fruit. Prayer drives one toward this specific end. In fact, without prayer, no change in moral character is ever possible. This marvelous change is brought to pass through earnest, persistent, faithful prayer.

Any assumed form of Christianity that does not cause this change in the hearts of people is a delusion and a snare.

DEAR LORD, I want to thank You and praise
You for the mercy and grace You show me. Amen.

Complete Surrender

I consider everything a loss compared to the surpassing greatness of knowing Christ Jesus my Lord, for whose sake I have lost all things. I consider them rubbish, that I may gain Christ.

Philippians 3:8

Consecration is the voluntary dedication of oneself to God. It is the setting apart of all we are, all we have, and all we expect to have or be. God must always come first.

It is not so much the giving of ourselves to the church. We must focus our eyes on God; He is the Source of all consecration. It is a separation of oneself to God, a devoting of all that He is and has to a sacred use.

Consecration has a sacred nature. It is devoted to holy ends. It is putting yourself willingly into God's hands to be used sacredly, with sanctifying ends in view.

LORD, I devote my life and all that I am to You today. I choose this day to serve You. Amen.

Separation for Holy Use

Let us draw near to God with a sincere heart in full assurance of faith, having our hearts sprinkled to cleanse us from a guilty conscience and having our bodies washed with pure water.

Hebrews 10:22

Consecration is much more than setting oneself apart from sinful things. It is living a holy live as opposed to a worldly life. It is living a life that is devoted to God and His purpose for you. It is devoting all we have to God for His use.

The consecration that meets God's demands is a complete consecration, with no mental reservation. To make a half-hearted, partial consecration is to make no consecration at all.

It involves our whole being, all we have and all that we are. Everything is definitely and willingly placed in God's hands for His supreme use.

GOD, I place all that I am in Your hands. I want my life to be fully set apart for Your plans and purposes. Amen.

Bad Praying = Bad Living

"I will hide My eyes from you;
even if you offer many prayers, I will
not listen. Your hands are full of blood."

Isaiah 1:15

Bad living means bad praying and, in the end, no praying at all. The stream of prayer cannot rise higher than the fountain of living.

We simply cannot talk strongly, intimately and confidently to God unless we are faithfully and truly living for Him. Our quiet time before God cannot become sanctified if our lives are not familiar with His laws and purposes.

We must learn this lesson well. Righteous character and Christlike conduct give us a peculiar and favored standing in prayer before God.

The Word places special emphasis on the part that our behavior plays on the value of our prayers.

GOD, successful prayer goes hand in hand with a life that pleases You. If there is any offensive way in me, lead me in the way everlasting. Amen.

Self-Sanctification

"Consecrate yourselves and be holy, because
I am the Lord your God. Keep My decrees and
follow them. I am the Lord, who makes you holy."

Leviticus 20:7-8

Here we are told to sanctify ourselves, and then in the next sentence we are taught that it is the Lord who sanctifies us.

Here is the two-fold meaning of sanctification, and a distinction that you always need to keep in mind. God does not consecrate us to His service; we must wholeheartedly commit or consecrate ourselves to Him. But we do not sanctify ourselves – it is the work of the Spirit in us.

Consecration is the intentional act of the believer and is the direct result of prayer. No prayerless person can ever understand the idea of full consecration.

GOD, I commit myself to You. Sanctify me through the work of Your indwelling Spirit. I cannot do this on my own. Amen.

Consecrated People

"Do you not know that your body is a
temple of the Holy Spirit, who is in you,
whom you have received from God? You are
not your own; you were bought at a price."

1 Corinthians 6:19-20

A life without prayer and consecration have nothing in common. A life of prayer naturally leads to
full consecration. Consecration fully recognizes
God's ownership of us. Praying shapes consecrated
people.

As prayer brings forth full consecration, so prayer
entirely influences a consecrated life. The prayer life
and the consecrated life are intimate companions.
They are Siamese twins, inseparable. Prayer enters
into every phase of a consecrated life. A life without
prayer that claims consecration is false.

GOD, thank You, for the gift of prayer and
that our prayers offered to You can produce a
consecrated life. Amen.

On Praying Ground

"No one can serve two masters. Either he
will hate the one and love the other, or he
will be devoted to the one and despise the
other. You cannot serve both God and money."

Matthew 6:24

Consecration is really devoting oneself to a life
of prayer. It means not only to pray, but to pray
consistently and effectively.

God cannot deny the requests of the man who
has completely dedicated himself to God and His
service. This act of the consecrated man puts him
on praying ground and pleading terms with God.

It puts him in reach of God. It places him where
he can get hold of God, and where he can influence
God to do things that He would not otherwise do.

ALMIGHTY GOD, Thank You, that our prayers
can move You. I devote myself to You today.
Amen.

Complete Surrender

When you ask, you do not receive, because
you ask with wrong motives, that you may
spend what you get on your pleasures.

James 4:3

God can depend on consecrated people. God can
afford to commit Himself to those who have fully
committed themselves to Him in prayer. He who
gives all to God will get all from God.

As prayer is the condition of full consecration,
so prayer is the habit, the rule, of him who has
dedicated himself wholly to God. Prayer is the most
appropriate thing in the consecrated life.

Prayer is part of the consecrated life. Prayer is the
constant, the inseparable, the intimate companion
of consecration. They walk and talk together.

DEAR FATHER GOD, thank You that I can
know that if I give my all to You, I will get all from
You. Amen.

Consecrated Service

To rescue us from the hand of our enemies,
and to enable us to serve Him without fear in
holiness and righteousness before Him all our days.

Luke 1:74-75

God wants consecrated followers because they can pray and will pray. He can use consecrated people because He can use praying people. Consecration and prayer meet in the same person.

Prayer is the tool with which the consecrated person works. The prime purpose of consecration is not service in the ordinary sense of the word. Consecration aims at the right sort of service, the scriptural kind.

It seeks to serve God, but in an entirely different way from that which is in the minds of church leaders and workers.

DEAR GOD, I want to be a praying servant of You so that You can use me in Your service. I want to live holy and righteous before You. Amen.

Living Right

Do everything without complaining or arguing,
so that you may become blameless and pure,
children of God without fault in a crooked and
depraved generation, in which you shine like stars
in the universe as you hold out the Word of life.

Philippians 2:14-16

In the Epistles, the focus is not on church activities,
but rather on the personal life.

It is good behavior, righteous conduct, godly conversation, holy living and a controlled temper –
things that belong primarily to the personal life in
religion.

Religion directs one to right living. Religion shows
itself in life. In this way religion proves its reality, its
sincerity and its divinity.

FATHER GOD, make me a shining star in Your
universe so that I may boast on the day of Christ
that I did not labor for nothing. But to receive the
crown of glory and eternal life from You. Amen.

A Holy Life

But you are not to be like that. Instead, the
greatest among you should be like the youngest,
and the one who rules like the one who serves.

Luke 22:26

The first aim of consecration is holiness of heart and
of life. It is to glorify God by a holy life flowing from
a heart cleansed from all sin.

To cultivate this kind of life and heart, one must
be watchful, one must pray and be forgiving toward
others. A true Christian seeks holiness of heart, he is
not satisfied without it.

For this very purpose he consecrates himself to
God. He gives himself entirely over to God in order
to be holy in heart and in life.

GOD, holiness of heart and life satisfy You.
Cleanse me from all unrighteousness for Your
glory. Amen.

Consecration and Holiness

Commit your way to the LORD;
trust in Him and He will do this. He will make
your righteousness shine like the dawn.

Psalm 37:5-6

Holiness of heart is thoroughly inspired by prayer. It takes prayer to bring one into such a consecrated life of holiness to the Lord.

Holy people are praying people. Holiness of heart and life encourage people to pray. Those who are unfamiliar with praying in solitude are not at all interested in consecration and holiness. Holiness thrives in the place of secret prayer.

In solitary prayer, holiness is found. Consecration brings forth holiness of heart, and prayer stands by when this is done.

ALMIGHTY GOD, I commit all my ways to You so that You may lift me up in due time and make me holy like You are holy. Amen.

The Best Hours of the Day

One of those days Jesus went out to a mountainside
to pray, and spent the night praying to God.

Luke 6:12

To pray is the greatest thing we can do; and to do it
well there must be calmness, time, and deliberation.
Otherwise, it is degraded into something small and
insignificant.

We cannot do too much real praying. If we want
to learn the wondrous art, we must not offer a
fragment here and there – "A little talk with Jesus," as
the chorus goes. But we must demand and hold the
best hours of the day for God and prayer, or there
will be no praying worth the name.

MY LORD AND MY GOD, I want to give the
best hours of every day to You. Please help me to
set my priorities straight. Amen.

The Lost Art of Prayer

Brothers, pray for us.

1 Thessalonians 5:25

In the hustle and bustle of life today people don't take time to pray. There are laymen who will give their money, but they will not give themselves to prayer.

There are plenty of preachers who will preach on the need of revival and the spread of the Kingdom of God. But there are many who will do that without prayer which makes all the preaching worthless.

To many people prayer is out of date; almost a lost art. The greatest benefactor that this age could have is the person who will bring the preachers and the church back to prayer.

★　★　★

GOD, in this busy age today, people have little time for anything. I want to make time for You, because I can't go one day without You. Amen.

The Spirit's Call

In the same way, the Spirit helps us in our
weakness. We do not know what we ought
to pray for, but the Spirit Himself intercedes
for us with groans that words cannot express.

Romans 8:26

The apostles only grasped a little bit of the great
importance of prayer before Pentecost. But the
Spirit coming at Pentecost elevated prayer to its
vital position in the gospel of Christ.

The call of prayer to every saint is the Spirit's most
urgent call. Sainthood's piety is made and perfected
by prayer. Where are the Christlike leaders who can
teach the modern saints how to pray?

An increase in educational facilities and a great
increase in money will be the direct curse to Christianity if they are not sanctified by more and better
praying than we are doing.

O GOD, I thank You for giving us Your Holy Spirit
who helps us in our weaknesses. When we don't
know what to pray, He prays for us. Amen.

Praying Leaders have Praying Followers

In all my prayers for all of you, I always pray with joy.

Philippians 1:4

Increased prayer will not happen as a matter of course. Only praying leaders can have praying followers.

Praying apostles will produce praying saints. We greatly need somebody who can set the saints to this business of praying. Who will restore this breach? He who can set the church to praying will be the greatest of reformers and apostles.

If this is realized, our prayers, faith, lives, and ministry will take on such a radical and aggressive form that it will bring about spiritual revival in people and in the church.

★ ★ ★

FATHER, thank You for praying leaders. Please guide the leaders in our church to bring people back to You and back to praying. Amen.

Changing the World

"Ask the Lord of the harvest, therefore,
to send out workers into His harvest field."

Matthew 9:38

God can work wonders if He has a suitable man. People can work wonders if they let God lead them. The full gift of the Spirit which turned the world upside-down would be useful in these days.

People who can stir things mightily for God, whose spiritual revolutions change the whole aspect of things, are the universal need of the church.

The church has never been without these people. They are the standing miracles of the divinity of the church. Their example and history are an unfailing inspiration and blessing. We should pray that such people would increase in number and power.

★ ★ ★

FATHER GOD, I pray today, that men and women who can stir things mightily for Your good purposes will increase in number and power in the world. Amen.

Doing Great Things for God

"I tell you the truth, anyone who has faith in Me
will do what I have been doing. He will do even greater
things than these, because I am going to the Father."

John 14:12

The past has not exhausted the possibilities or the
demands of doing great things for God. The church
that is dependent on its past history for its miracles
of power and grace is a fallen church.

God wants people who look to Him with pure
hearts. People who are willing to sacrifice self and
the world in order to do God's will.

Let us pray that God's promises to prayer may be
more than realized.

DEAR GOD, I thank You that I can do great
things by believing in Your Word and holding on
to Your promises. Amen.

Faith in Action

"Whoever has My commands and obeys
them, he is the one who loves Me."

John 14:21

Unquestionably, obedience is a high virtue, the quality of a soldier. A soldier has to be obedient. This obedience must be without questioning or complaining. Obedience is faith in action. It is the outflow, the very test of love.

The gift of the Holy Spirit in full measure and in richer experience depends on loving obedience. Obedience to God is a condition of spiritual abundance, inward satisfaction and stability of heart.

Obedience opens the gates of the Holy City and gives access to the Tree of Life.

DEAR HEAVENLY FATHER, I want to be obedient to You with all my heart and soul. I know that obedience opens the gate for the gift of Your Holy Spirit. Amen.

Our Destination

Therefore let us leave the elementary teachings
about Christ and go on to maturity.

Hebrews 6:1

It is essential, in our Christian walk, that we have
something definite in view and that we strike out for
that one goal.

It is important that we do not lose sight of the
starting point in a religious life, and that we measure
the steps already walked.

But it is likewise necessary to keep the end in view
and that the steps required to reach the standard are
always in sight.

DEAR GOD, my eyes are fixed on You, the
Author and Perfecter of my faith. Please help me
to never lose sight of You. Amen.

Keeping All the Commandments

"Oh, that their hearts would be inclined to fear Me and keep all My commands always, so that it might go well with them and their children forever."

Deuteronomy 5:29

The keeping of all God's commandments is the demonstration of the obedience that God requires from us. Can a believer receive help to obey every one of them? Of course. All that a person needs to do is pray.

Does God give commandments that we cannot obey? No. In all of Scripture, not a single instance is recorded of God having commanded any man to do a thing that was beyond his power.

Is God so inconsiderate to require of man something that he is unable to do? Certainly not. That is against God's character.

DEAR LORD GOD, You will not let me be tempted beyond what I can bear. Amen.

Our Heavenly Parent

"If you, then, though you are evil,
know how to give good gifts to your children,
how much more will your Father in heaven
give good gifts to those who ask Him!"

Matthew 7:11

Think about this thought for a moment. Do earthly parents require their children to perform duties that they cannot do? What father would be so unjust and mean? Are our earthly parents kinder, better, more just than our perfect God?

In principle, obedience to God is the same quality as obedience to earthly parents. It implies the giving up of one's own way to follow that of another. It implies the submission of oneself to the authority and requirements of a parent.

LOVING FATHER, I submit myself to Your authority and give up my own ways to obey You. You are a perfect God, and deserve the best from us. Guide me in obedience today. Amen.

It Pays to Be Obedient

"You may ask Me for anything in
My name, and I will do it. If you love Me,
you will obey what I command."

John 14:14-15

Commands, either from our heavenly Father or our earthly father, are directed by love. All such commands are in the best interests of those who are commanded. God has issued His commands to us in order to make us prosper.

It pays, therefore, to be obedient. Obedience brings its own reward. God has made it so. Since He has, we can know that He would never ask us to do anything that we aren't capable of doing, or that we can't do.

Obedience is love fulfilling every command. It is love expressing itself.

DEAR FATHER GOD, I know that You give us commands in order to make us prosper. Thank You, Lord, that I may know that You reward obedience. Amen.

At God's Disposal

Then there will be righteous sacrifices,
whole burnt offerings to delight You;
then bulls will be offered on Your altar.

Psalm 51:19

Prayer leads to full consecration. Consecration is but the silent expression of prayer. The prayer life is the direct fruit of entire consecration to God.

No consecration is pleasing to God that is not perfect in all its parts. Consecration is putting oneself entirely at the disposal of God. And God wants and commands all His consecrated ones to be praying people.

This is the one definite standard at which we must aim. We cannot afford to seek anything lower than this.

GOD, my aim today is to be fully consecrated to You. I surrender myself completely to You – use me for Your divine purposes. Amen.

Supplies of Grace

The law is holy, and the commandment
is holy, righteous and good.

Romans 7:12

It is really much easier to please God than to please people. Moreover, we can *know* when we please Him. This is the witness of the Spirit – the inward, divine assurance given to all the children of God that they are doing their Father's will and that their ways are well pleasing in His sight.

God's commandments, then, can be obeyed by all who seek supplies of grace to enable them to obey. These commandments must be obeyed. God's government is at stake.

The spirit of rebellion is the very essence of sin. It is the denial of God's authority that He cannot tolerate.

HEAVENLY FATHER I ask for Your grace to help me obey Your commands. Amen.

God's Enabling Act

For God did not give us a spirit of timidity,
but a spirit of power, of love and of self-discipline.

2 Timothy 1:7

If anyone complains that man under the Fall is too weak to obey, the answer is that, through the Atonement of Christ, man is able to obey.

The Atonement is God's enabling act. God works in us, through regeneration and the Holy Spirit, giving us grace that is sufficient. This grace is furnished without measure in answer to prayer.

So, while God commands, He stands pledged to give us all the necessary strength to meet His demands. Because this is true, man has no excuse for disobedience. He may serve the Lord with reverence and godly fear.

DEAR GOD, because Christ died for us, and because You gave us Your Holy Spirit to comfort us, we are able to obey You and meet Your demands. Thank You, Father. Amen.

Partaker of the Divine Nature

"I desire to do Your will, O my God."

Psalm 40:8

Those who say it is impossible to keep God's commandments overlook one important consideration.

It is the vital truth that, through prayer and faith, man's nature is changed and made a partaker of the divine nature. The inability to keep God's commandments because of a weak, fallen state is removed.

By this radical change in moral nature, a believer receives power to obey God in every way. Because of this, rebellion is removed and is replaced by a heart that gladly obeys God's Word.

★ ★ ★

O GOD, I desire to do Your will. Thank You that through faith and prayer, we receive power and strength to obey. Amen.

Boldness Before the Throne

Who may ascend the hill of the LORD? He who has clean hands and a pure heart, who does not lift up his soul to an idol or swear by what is false.

Psalm 24:3-4

Obedience can ask with boldness at the throne of grace.

The disobedient person is timid in his approach and hesitant in his supplication. Such a person is stopped by his wrongdoing. The requesting, obedient child comes into the presence of his Father with confidence and boldness. Obedience frees one from the dread of acting disobediently and instead, gives courage.

To do God's will without hesitation is the joy and the privilege of the successful praying man. He who has clean hands and a pure heart can pray with confidence.

FATHER, I want to experience the joy of successful praying by doing Your will without hesitation. Guide me through Your Spirit. Amen.

The Christian's Trade

Search me, O God, and know my heart;
test me and know my anxious thoughts.
See if there is any offensive way in me,
and lead me in the way everlasting.

Psalm 139:23-24

"The Christian's trade," said Martin Luther, "is prayer." But the Christian has another trade to learn before he proceeds to learn the secrets of the trade of prayer. He must learn perfect obedience to the Father's will. Obedience follows love, and prayer follows obedience.

One who has been disobedient may pray. A person may come to God's feet with tears, confession, and a heart full of regret.

God will hear him and answer his prayer.

★　★　★

GOD, I want to obey You. Search me, O God, and know my heart. Lead me in the way everlasting. Amen.

An Obedient Life

We have confidence before God and receive
from Him everything we ask, because we
obey His commands and do what pleases Him.

1 John 3:21-22

A life of obedience helps prayer. It speeds prayer to the throne. God cannot help hearing the prayer of an obedient child. Unquestioning obedience counts much in the sight of God at the throne of heavenly grace.

It acts like the flowing tides of many rivers. An obedient life is not simply a reformed life. It is not the old life primed and repainted. It is not a superficial churchgoing life or a flurry of activities.

Neither is it only an external conformation to what society expects. It takes much more than this to be a truly obedient Christian.

★ ★ ★

DEAR LORD GOD, I know that it pleases You when we are obedient to You. Please guide me so that I may hear Your voice more clearly. Amen.

Free Access to God

May God Himself, the God of peace, sanctify
you through and through. May your whole spirit,
soul and body be kept blameless at the
coming of our Lord Jesus Christ.

1 Thessalonians 5:23

A life of full obedience, a life that is focused on God,
will not be distracted by any obstacles when praying.

If you have an earnest desire to pray well, you
must learn to obey well. If you have a desire to learn
to pray, then you must have an earnest desire to
learn how to do God's will.

If you want to have free access to God in prayer,
then every obstacle in the nature of sin or disobedience must be removed.

God delights in the prayers of obedient children.

FATHER GOD, through obedience to You, we
can ask for anything in Your name, and You will
do it. I praise Your holy name. Amen.

Baptizing Tears

The Spirit Himself intercedes
for us with groans that words cannot express.

Romans 8:26

Requests coming from the lips of those who delight to do God's will, reach His ears with great speed. God answers them promptly.

In themselves, tears are not rewarding. Yet, they have their uses in prayer. Tears should baptize our place of supplication. The person who has never wept over his sins has never really prayed. Tears, sometimes, are a prodigal's only plea. But tears are for the past; for sin and wrongdoing.

There is another step and stage waiting to be taken. That step is unquestioning obedience. Until it is taken, prayer for blessing and continued sustenance will be of no use.

HEAVENLY FATHER, I ask You to please forgive my sins and have mercy on me. Thank You for Your Holy Spirit that intercedes for us. Amen.

Shaping Character

The LORD detests men of perverse heart but
He delights in those whose ways are blameless.

Proverbs 11:20

Much of the feebleness of religion results from the failure to have a scriptural standard in religion by which to shape character. This largely results from the omission of prayer or the failure to emphasize the importance of prayer.

We cannot determine our spiritual growth if we have nothing to measure it against. There must always be something definite before the mind's eye at which we are aiming and to which we are driving.

Neither can there be inspiration if there is nothing greater to stimulate us.

FATHER GOD, let my only aim be to become more and more like Jesus every day. Amen.

The Sweetest Experience

Be joyful always; pray continually; give thanks
in all circumstances, for this is God's
will for you in Christ Jesus.

1 Thessalonians 5:16-18

Many Christians are without purpose because they have nothing on which to shape their conduct and character.

There is nothing to keep them focused, determined and on the right path. Prayer helps one gain a clearer, more focused idea of religion.

In fact, prayer itself is a very definite thing; it aims at something specific, it has a mark at which it aims. Prayer aims at the most definite, the highest, and the sweetest religious experience.

GOD, thank You, for giving us Your Word upon which we can shape our lives. Lord, You give purpose and meaning to our lives. Amen.

Wanting All of God

I thank God, whom I serve, as my forefathers
did, with a clear conscience, as night and
day I constantly remember you in my prayers.

2 Timothy 1:3

Praying people want all that God has in store for them. They are not satisfied with a low religious life; superficial, vague, and indefinite.

Praying people constantly strive for more. They are not after being saved from some sin, but saved from all sin, both inward and outward.

They are not only after deliverance from sinning, but from sin itself, from its being, its power, and its pollution. They are after holiness of heart and life.

DEAR LORD GOD, I want to receive all that You have in store for me. Please help me to pray without ceasing. Amen.

The Religious Life

What is more, I consider everything a loss compared
to the surpassing greatness of knowing Christ
Jesus my Lord, for whose sake I have lost all things.
I consider them rubbish, that I may gain Christ.

Philippians 3:8

Prayer believes in and seeks for the very highest
religious life set before us in the Word of God. When
we make our own standards, there is delusion and
falsity for our desires, convenience and pleasure
form the rule, and that is always a fleshly and a low
rule.

From it, all the fundamental principles of a
Christ-centered religion are left out. When we allow
others to set our standard of religion, it is gene-
rally deficient because, valuable virtues may be lost,
whilst defects are carried through.

GOD, I pray for Your help in setting my standard
of religion. I consider all things a loss, that I may
gain Christ. Amen.

Religious Opinions

He gave Himself for us to redeem us from all
wickedness and to purify for Himself a people that
are His very own, eager to do what is good.

Titus 2:14

The most serious damage in determining what religion is according to what others say, is in allowing current opinion to shape our religious character.

Commonplace religion is pleasing to flesh and blood. There is no self-denial in it. It is good enough for our neighbors. Others are living on a low plane, on a compromising level, living as the world lives. Why should we be different – striving for good works? But, are the easy-going crowds who are living prayerless lives going to heaven?

Is heaven a fit place for non-praying, ease-loving people? That is the supreme question.

★   ★   ★

DEAR LORD JESUS, You are the Way and the Truth and the Life – the way to heaven. Amen.

The Divine Rule

We, however, will not boast beyond proper limits,
but will continue our boasting to the field God
has assigned to us, a field that reaches even to you.

2 Corinthians 10:13

No standard of religion is worth a moment's consideration when it neglects prayer. No standard is worth any thought that does not make prayer the main thing in religion. A life of prayer is the divine rule.

This is the pattern, just as our Lord is the one Example that we must follow. Prayer is required for a spiritual life. It is God's standard at which we are aiming, not man's.

Our goal should be set not by the opinions of people, not by what they say, but by what the Scriptures say.

FATHER, I know that the divine rule is to live a life of prayer and obedience before You. I press on to reach the goal for which You have called me. Amen.

Full Consecration

Offer your bodies as living sacrifices,
holy and pleasing to God.

Romans 12:1

A low standard of religion lives by a low standard of praying.

Everything in our religious lives depends upon being definite. The definiteness of our religious experiences and of our living will depend on the definiteness of our views of what religion is and of the things of which it consists. There is only one way to be fully consecrated to God.

A full renunciation of self, and a sincere offering of all to God – this is the divine requirement. There is nothing vague in that. Nothing in that is governed by the opinions of others or affected by how people live around us.

DEAR GOD, I surrender my life to You completely. I want to live a holy and pleasing life in Your sight. Please guide me. Amen.

Obeying Because of Love

Receive from Him anything we ask, because
we obey His commands and do what pleases Him.

1 John 3:22

Love delights to obey and please whom it loves.
There are no hardships in love.

There may be demands, but no irritations. This is
obedience, running ahead of every command. It is
love, obeying by anticipation.

Those who say that men are bound to commit
sin because of environment, heredity, or tendency
are very wrong. Far be it from our heavenly Father to
demand impossibilities of His children. It is possible
to please Him in all things, for He is not hard to
please.

Thank God it is possible for every child of God to
please our heavenly Father!

★ ★ ★

LORD, thank You, for not expecting the
impossible from us. I know that I can do all things
through You who gives me strength. Amen.

Experiencing religion

My dear friends, as you have always obeyed –
not only in my presence, but now much more in my
absence – continue to work out your salvation with
fear and trembling, for it is God who works in you
to will and to act according to His good purpose.

Philippians 2:12-13

A scriptural standard of religion includes a clear religious experience. Religion involves experience. The new birth is a definite Christian experience.

The witness of the Spirit is not a vague *something*, but an inward assurance given by the Holy Spirit that we are the children of God. In fact, everything belonging to religious experience is clear, bringing conscious joy, peace and love.

This is the divine standard of religion, a standard attained by constant prayer and a religious experience kept alive and enlarged by the same means of prayer.

GOD, I thank You, for the inward assurance that I am Your child. Amen.

Doing God's Will

For whoever keeps the whole law and yet stumbles
at just one point is guilty of breaking all of it.

James 2:10

What is obedience? It is doing God's will. How many
of the commandments require obedience? To keep
half of them and break the other half – is that real
obedience? To keep all the commandments but one
– is that obedience?

The spirit that prompts a man to break one commandment is the spirit that may move him to break
them all. God's commandments are a unit. To break
one strikes at the principle that underlies and runs
through the whole.

He who does not hesitate to break a single commandment probably would, under the same stress
and surrounded by the same circumstances, break
them all.

★ ★ ★

LORD GOD, I know that by the help of Your
indwelling Spirit, it is possible to obey Your laws.
You are worthy of our praise. Amen.

Prayer Generates Love

For you have been born again, not
of perishable seed, but of imperishable,
through the living and enduring word of God.

1 Peter 1:23

Prayer invariably generates a love for the Word of God. Prayer leads people to obey the Word of God and puts an unspeakable joy into the obedient heart.

Praying people and Bible-reading people are the same kind of people. The God of the Bible and the God of prayer are one. God speaks to man in the Bible; man speaks to God in prayer. One reads the Bible to discover God's will and prays in order to receive power to do that will.

Bible reading and praying are the distinguishing traits of those who strive to know and please God.

DEAR GOD, guide me in my prayers to You and in my Bible reading so that I may discover Your will. Amen.

A Church-Supporting Spirit

> Let us not give up meeting together,
> as some are in the habit of doing.

Hebrews 10:25

Just as prayer generates a love for the Scriptures and causes people to begin to read the Bible, so does prayer also cause men and women to visit the house of God to hear the Scriptures explained.

Churchgoing is closely connected with the Bible, primarily because the Bible cautions us against not giving up meeting together. Churchgoing also results because God's chosen minister explains and enforces the Scriptures upon his hearers. Prayer develops a resolve in those who practice it to not forsake the church.

Prayer generates a churchgoing conscience, a church-loving heart, and a church-supporting spirit. Praying people take delight in the preaching of the Word and the support of the church.

FATHER, help us to meet and pray together with other believers. Amen.

Protection Against Sinning

I have hidden Your word in my heart
that I might not sin against You.

Psalm 119:11

Psalm 119 is a directory of God's Word. With three or four exceptions, each verse contains a word that identifies or locates the Word of God. Quite often, the psalmist knelt in supplication, praying several times.

Here, in verse 11, the psalmist found his protection against sin – by having God's Word hidden in his heart and his whole being filled with that Word.

We find that the power of prayer creates a real love for the Scriptures and puts within people a nature that will take pleasure in the Word.

★ ★ ★

HEAVENLY FATHER, by having Your Word hidden in my heart I know that I can be protected from doing wrong. Amen.

Jesus, a Man of Prayer

He went to Nazareth, where He had been
brought up, and on the Sabbath day He went
into the Synagogue, as was His custom.

Luke 4:16

Do we relish God's Word? If so, then let us give ourselves continually to prayer.

He who would have a heart for the reading of the
Bible must not – dare not – forget to pray. A person
who loves the Bible will also love to pray. A person
who loves to pray will delight in the law of the Lord.

Our Lord was a man of prayer. He magnified the
Word of God and often quoted the Scriptures. Right
through His earthly life, Jesus observed Sabbath
keeping, churchgoing, and the reading of the Word
of God. His prayer intermingled with them all.

DEAR FATHER, I give myself continually to You
in prayer. Make me more and more like Jesus every
day. Amen.

A Secret Place

"When you pray, go into your room,
close the door and pray to your Father,
who is unseen. Then your Father, who sees
what is done in secret, will reward you."

Matthew 6:6

Let it be said that no two things are more essential to a Spirit-filled life than Bible reading and prayer.

They will help you to grow in grace, to obtain joy from living a Christian life, and to be established in the way of eternal peace. Neglecting these things paves the way for a life without purpose.

Reading God's Word regularly and praying habitually in a secret place of the Most High, puts one where one is absolutely safe from the attacks of the Enemy of souls. It guarantees a person salvation and final victory through the overcoming power of the Lamb.

GOD, thank You that I can live a life of victory because You have already overcome the world. Amen.

Fullness and Boldness

"Stay in the city until you have
been clothed with power from on high."

Luke 24:49

Without question the early church received the
Lord's teaching that prayer is answered.

The certainty of the answer to prayer was as fixed
as God's Word is true. The Holy Spirit came because
the disciples put their faith into practice. They
waited in the Upper Room in prayer for ten days,
and the promise was fulfilled. The answer came just
as Jesus said.

The answer to prayer was a response to their faith
and prayer. The fullness of the Spirit always brings
patience and boldness.

LOVING FATHER, thank You, that You always
know best what we need. Thank You for giving us
Your Holy Spirit. Amen.

Pray in Seasons of Conflict

Pray in the Spirit on all occasions
with all kinds of prayers and requests.

Ephesians 6:18

The description of the Christian soldier given by Paul in Ephesians 6 is compact and comprehensive. He is seen as always being in the seasons of conflict.

There are seasons of prosperity and adversity, victory and defeat. He is to pray in all seasons and with all prayer. This is to be added to the armor when he goes into battle. The Christian soldier, if he fights to win, must pray fervently.

Only in this way is he able to defeat his long-standing enemy, the Devil, and his many agents. To pray on all occasions is the divine direction given to all Christ's soldiers.

DEAR GOD, I know that I am more than a conqueror through Christ's love for us. I must only pray if I want to win the battle. Help me please. Amen.

Idle Church Members

In the name of the Lord Jesus Christ,
we command you, brothers, to keep away
from every brother who does not live according
to the teaching you received from us.

2 Thessalonians 3:6

As good as the church at Thessalonica was, it also needed instruction and caution on this matter of looking after those who did not live according to the teachings.

It is not the mere presence of idle persons in a church that causes God's displeasure. It is when they are tolerated and no steps are taken to either cure them of their evil practices, or exclude them from the fellowship of the church. This carelessness regarding the wayward members on the part of the church is but a sad sign of a lack of praying.

FATHER, guide us, Your church, to not neglect those who are not living according to Your teachings. Let us be a helping hand to them in turning back to You. Amen.

— 155 —

A Believer's Walk

Endure hardship with us
like a good soldier of Christ Jesus.

2 Timothy 2:3

What a misconception many people have of the Christian life! The average church member today does not seem to know anything about conflict or how the world, the Devil and flesh will try to hinder a believer's walk.

It is just at this point in today's Christianity that one may find its greatest defect. There is little or nothing of the soldier element in it. The discipline, self-denial, spirit of hardship and determination so prominent in and belonging to the military life, are lacking.

Yet the Christian life is warfare. We need to fight the good fight and endure hardships as good soldiers of Christ.

ALMIGHTY FATHER, please strengthen me to endure hardships of many kinds like a good soldier of Christ. Amen.

Disorderly Conduct

Brothers, if someone is caught in a sin, you who
are spiritual should restore him gently.

Galatians 6:1

The church is an organization for mutual help,
and it is charged with the watchful care of all of its
members. Unruly behavior cannot pass by unnoticed.

The work of the church is not just to seek members, but to watch over and guard them after they
have entered the church. If someone starts following
the path of sin, members of the church should try to
redirect that person to God's way.

However, if someone knowingly chooses to
sin, then that person should be removed from the
church. This is the doctrine our Lord lays down for
us, His church.

HEAVENLY FATHER, I pray, that people shall
see Your church as a safe haven and a place of rest
and comfort. Guide Your church in their work to
guard and watch over Your people. Amen.

Supplication

Pray in the Spirit on all occasions with all kinds
of prayers and requests. With this in mind,
be alert and always keep on praying for all the saints.

Ephesians 6:18

The power of prayer is most forceful on the battle-field in the midst of the noise and strife of conflict. Paul was pre-eminently a soldier of the cross. His strength was almost gone. What reinforcements could he count on?

It was a critical moment in the conflict. What strength could be added to the energy of his own prayers? The answer lies in the prayers of others; his fellow believers.

These, he believed, will bring him additional aid. He could then win his fight, overcome his adversaries, and, ultimately, prevail.

★ ★ ★

LOVING FATHER, in the midst of the hustle-and-bustle, I become still before You. Refresh my soul, strengthen my faith and help me fight the good fight for Your glory. Amen.

Selfish Praying

When you ask, you do not receive, because
you ask with wrong motives, that you may
spend what you get on your pleasures.

James 4:3

The soldier's prayer must reflect his profound concern for the success and well-being of the whole army. The battle is not altogether a personal matter.

Victory cannot be achieved for self alone. The cause of God, His saints, their woes and trials, their duties and crosses, all should find a pleading voice in the Christian soldier when he prays.

He dare not limit his praying to himself. Selfish praying is the quickest way to dry up spiritual blessings. Pray with God's whole army and His perfect will in mind.

FATHER GOD, when I pray I want my motives to be pure and right. Please guide me when I pray not to pray selfish prayers, but to have Your perfect will in mind. Amen.

Watchfulness

"Watch and pray."

Matthew 26:41

The Christian soldier is compelled to constant guard duty. He is faced with an enemy who never sleeps, who is always alert, and who is ever prepared to take advantage of the fortunes of war.

Watchfulness is a fundamental principle of Christ's warriors. They cannot dare to be asleep at their posts. Such a lapse brings them not only under the displeasure of the Captain of their salvation, but also exposes them to added danger.

Watchfulness, therefore, is a necessity for a soldier of the Lord.

★ ★ ★

LORD, You tell us in Your Word to watch and pray so that we may not fall into temptation. Make me a worthy soldier of Your army. Amen.

Watch, Watch, Watch!

Pray in the Spirit on all occasions
with all kinds of prayers and requests.

Ephesians 6:18

In the New Testament, there are three different meanings for the word "watch." The first means "absence of sleep" and implies a wakeful frame of mind. The second meaning is to be "fully awake" – through carelessness or laziness, something horrible could suddenly happen. The third means "to be calm and collected in spirit," cautious against all pitfalls and distractions.

All three definitions are used by Paul. Two of them are used in connection with prayer. Watchfulness must guard and cover the whole spiritual man and prepare him for prayer. Everything resembling unpreparedness or non-vigilance is death to prayer.

FATHER, I realize that it is important to watch
and pray always because our enemy prowls
around like a hungry lion. Help me, Lord, to resist
the Devil. Amen.

Alert Soldiers

On reaching the place, He said to them,
"Pray that you will not fall into temptation."

Luke 22:40

The Christian soldier must be as intense in his praying as in his fighting, for his victories will depend much more on his praying than on his fighting.

Prayer and supplication must strengthen the armor of God. The Holy Spirit must aid the supplication with His own zealous plea. And the soldier must pray in the Spirit.

In this, as in all other forms of warfare, eternal vigilance is the price of victory. Thus, watchfulness and perseverance must mark every activity of the Christian warrior.

GOD, make me a Christian warrior who depends greatly on my prayers to You. Make me watchful and perseverant through the help of Your Spirit. Amen.

Intercession

"For where two or three come together
in My name, there am I with them."

Matthew 18:20

The pious Quesnel said that "God is found in union and agreement. Nothing is more efficacious than this in prayer."

Intercession combines with prayers and supplications. The word *intercession* does not necessarily mean "prayer in relation to others." It means "a coming together, a falling in with a most intimate friend for free, unrestrained communion."

It implies free prayer, familiar and bold. This passage represents the church in prayer. The strength of the church is in prayer.

LORD, thank You, for the knowledge we have that where two or three come together in Your name, You will be there with them. I praise Your holy name. Amen.

Church Discipline

"If he refuses to listen to them, tell it to the church,
treat him as you would a pagan or a tax collector."

Matthew 18:17

Discipline in church, now a lost art in the modern church, must go hand in hand with prayer. The church that has no disposition to separate wrongdoers from the church, will have no communication with God.

Church purity must precede the church's prayers. The unity of discipline in the church precedes the unity of prayers by the church. Take note of the fact that a church that is careless in discipline will be careless in praying.

The need of watchfulness over the lives of its members belongs to the church of God.

DEAR FATHER, I pray for Your churches around the world to not be careless in their disciplines so that their prayers will not become careless. Amen.

Fighting Qualities

*Therefore put on the full armor of God,
so that when the day of evil comes,
you may be able to stand your ground.*

Ephesians 6:13

The Christian soldier who is bent on defeating the Devil must possess a clear idea of the character of the life into which he has entered.

He must know something of his enemies – their strengths, their skills, their viciousness. Knowing something of the character of the enemy and realizing the need of preparation to overcome them, will be of great help to withstand the enemy when the day of evil comes.

How can the brave warrior for Christ be made braver still? Prayer, and more prayer, adds to the fighting qualities and the more certain victories of God's good, fighting people.

GOD, it is only through diligent prayer to You, that I can become a good, fighting soldier for You. Help me to never stop praying. Amen.

Godly Decline

"I know your deeds, your hard work
and your perseverance. I know that
you cannot tolerate wicked men."

Revelation 2:2

It is somewhat striking that the church at Ephesus,
though it had left its first love and had sadly declined
in vital godliness and in the things that make up
spiritual life, still received credit for this good quality
of not tolerating wicked men.

At the same time, the church at Pergamos was
given a warning because the beliefs of some members were stumbling blocks for other members.

The impression is that the church leaders were
blind to the presence of such hurtful characters.
There was no concerted prayer effort to cleanse the
church and keep it clean. A praying church should
be quick to help a fallen member.

DEAR GOD, I pray for Your churches to be
praying churches who are keen to help fellow
believers and lead and guide them. Amen.

Fighting the Good Fight

Fight the good fight of the faith.
Take hold of the eternal life to which you
were called when you made your good
confession in the presence of many witnesses.

1 Timothy 6:12

Christian soldiers, fighting the good fight of faith, have access to a place of retreat where they continually go to for prayer.

It cannot be said too often that the life of a Christian is warfare, an intense conflict, a lifelong contest. The Bible calls people to life, not a picnic or holiday. It requires effort, wrestling, and struggling. It demands full energy of the spirit to withstand the enemy and to come out, in the end, more than a conqueror.

It is not an easy rose-lined path. From start to finish, it is war.

LOVING FATHER, thank You, for giving rest and strength for our souls in the constant battle we are fighting. We are more than conquerors through Your great love for us. Amen.

Pray or Be Prey!

Be self-controlled and alert. Your enemy
the devil prowls around like a roaring lion
looking for someone to devour.

1 Peter 5:8

God's church is a militant host. It fights against unseen forces of evil. God's people form an army fighting to establish His Kingdom on the earth. Their aim is to destroy the sovereignty of Satan and, over its ruins, erect the kingdom of God.

The entire life of a Christian soldier is dependent on a life of prayer.

Without prayer – no matter what else he has – the Christian soldier's life will be feeble and ineffective. Without prayer, he is an easy prey for his spiritual enemies.

FATHER GOD, I don't want to be an easy target for the enemy. Help me to be self-controlled and alert, and to always come to You, for You renew my strength. Amen.

A Plentiful Harvest

"The harvest is plentiful but the workers are few.
Ask the Lord of the harvest, therefore, to send
out workers into His harvest field."

Matthew 9:37-38

We read in Scripture that our Lord had called His disciples aside to rest awhile, exhausted by the demands made on them.

But the crowds preceded Him, and instead of finding solitude, quiet, and rest, He found great multitudes eager to see, to hear, and to be healed. His compassionate heart was moved. The ripened harvests needed laborers.

He did not call these laborers all at once, but He encouraged the disciples to take themselves to God in prayer, asking Him to send forth laborers into His harvest.

DEAR FATHER, grant me a compassionate heart like Jesus. Help me to see ripened hearts that are ready to receive Your Son into their lives. Amen.

Church Export Products

"Your kingdom come, Your will
be done on earth as it is in heaven."

Matthew 6:10

The missionary movement in the apostolic church was born in an atmosphere of fasting and prayer. Missionary work is God's work.

Praying missionaries are needed for the work, and only a praying church can send them out. Prayer has the ability to make the spreading of the gospel so much more powerful.

The energy to give the gospel momentum and conquering power over all its enemies is the energy of prayer.

LORD, spreading Your gospel across the world depends on the prayers of Your children. Make us strong, and grant us the energy to make things happen through our prayers to You. Amen.

The Divine Plan

To the weak I became weak, to win the weak.
I have become all things to all men
so that by all possible means I might save some.

1 Corinthians 9:22

Our Lord's plan for securing workers in the missionary field is the same as His plan for obtaining preachers. It is through the process of praying.

It is the prayer plan as distinguished from all man-made plans. These mission workers are to be "sent people". God must send them. They are God-called, divinely moved to this great work. They are inwardly moved to enter the harvest fields of the world.

People do not choose to be missionaries any more than they choose to be preachers. God sends out laborers in His harvest fields in answer to the prayers of His church.

ALMIGHTY GOD, thank You, that You call missionaries to the harvest field in answer to the prayers of Your church. Amen.

Praying Missionaries

He saw that there was no one, he was
appalled that there was no one to intervene.

Isaiah 59:16

A praying church brings about laborers in the harvest field of the world. It is the church's responsibility to pray for missionaries.

It is all right to send trained people to the foreign field, but first of all they must be God-sent. The sending is the fruit of prayer. As praying people pray for workers to be sent, so in turn the workers themselves must be praying people. The prime mission of these praying missionaries is to convert prayerless, heathen people into praying people.

Prayer can help people fulfill their calling, their divine credentials, and their work.

GOD, my prayer today is for all the missionaries out in the field spreading Your Word. Bless them and keep them and grant them Your peace. Amen.

No Harvests without Prayer

"Ask the Lord of the harvest, therefore,
to send out workers into His harvest field."

Matthew 9:38

The church is urged to pray for laborers to be sent into the harvest of the Lord. The scarcity of laborers in the harvest field is due to the fact that the church fails to pray for laborers as Jesus commanded.

God's chosen laborers are the only ones who will truly go, filled with Christlike compassion and Christlike power.

Christ's people on their knees, with Christ's compassion in their hearts for dying people and for needy souls, is the pledge of laborers in numbers and character to meet the needs of earth and the purposes of heaven.

LORD, here I am Your servant, on my knees before You. Use me to touch the souls of people in need of You. Amen.

Fuel for Life

"It is written: 'Man does not live
on bread alone, but on every word that
comes from the mouth of God.'"

Matthew 4:4

The Word of God is put into action by the process
and practice of prayer. If it is written in our hearts, it
will form an outflowing current of prayer.

Promises, stored in the heart, are the fuel from
which prayer receives life and warmth. Just as coal
which has been stored in the earth gives us comfort
on stormy days and cold nights, the Word of God
stored in our hearts is the food by which prayer is
nourished and strengthened.

Prayer, like people, cannot live by bread alone.

DEAR HEAVENLY FATHER, I know that I
cannot live on bread alone, but rather on every
word that comes from Your mouth. Amen.

God's Truth

Do you show contempt for the riches of His kindness, tolerance and patience, not realizing that God's kindness leads you toward repentance?

Romans 2:4

God holds all good in His hands. That good comes to us through our Lord Jesus Christ, only because of His atoning sacrifice and by asking it in His name.

God is so much involved in prayer and hearing and answering that all His attributes and His whole being are centered in that great fact. It distinguishes Him as wonderfully good, and powerfully attractive in His nature.

God's truthfulness is at stake in the engagements to answer prayer. His wisdom, His truth, and His goodness are involved. God is Truth – and He always answers the prayers of His children who earnestly seek His name.

FATHER GOD, You are Truth. You always keep Your promises. May Your name be exalted over all the earth. Amen.

God's Ability to Do!

"If You can do anything, take pity on us and help us."

Mark 9:22

The only condition that restricts God's power making Him unable to act is a lack of faith. He is not limited in action nor restrained by the conditions that limit people. God is never limited.

The conditions of time, place, nearness, ability and all others that could possibly be named, have no bearing on God. If God's children will look to Him and cry to Him with true prayer, He will hear and will deliver, no matter how dire their circumstances.

It is strange how God has to school His people in His ability to do all things!

FATHER GOD, we are not restricted by time, place or ability to do great things for You. The only thing restricting us is our lack of prayer. Make me a praying warrior. Amen.

Above Human Thought

Now to Him who is able to do
immeasurably more than all we ask or imagine,
to Him be glory in the church and in Christ Jesus.

Ephesians 3:20-21

Prayer has to do with God, with His ability to do.

In God's ability to do, He goes far beyond man's ability to ask. Human thoughts, human words, human imaginations, human desires, and human needs cannot in any way measure God's ability to do.

Prayer goes forward by the power of God Himself. Prayer goes forth with faith, not only in the promise of God, but also in God Himself and in His ability to do.

LORD, I thank You, for the knowledge in Your Word that You are able to do immeasurably more than we can ask or imagine. To You be all the glory forever and ever. Amen.

The Majesty of God

"Forget the former things, do not dwell on the past."

Isaiah 43:18

Every day we see the majesty and power of God in His creation. This should be the basis of our faith in God and should help us in our prayers.

Then God calls us away from what He has done and turns our minds to Himself personally. The infinite glory and power of His person are set before us to meditate on.

Therefore, if we have prayer and faith, He will so answer our prayers and so work in us that His former work shall not be remembered. What lies ahead for us in God's plan will be much greater.

★ ★ ★

ALMIGHTY GOD, my prayer to You today is for increased faith and perseverance in prayer. I want to bring glory to You through my life. Amen.

The House of God

Let us not give up meeting together,
as some are in the habit of doing.

Hebrews 10:25

Without prayer, a church is like a body without spirit; it is a dead, lifeless thing. A church with prayer in it has God in it. When prayer is set aside, God is also set aside. When prayer becomes an unfamiliar exercise, then God Himself is a stranger there.

As God's house is a house of prayer, the divine intention is that people should leave their homes and go to meet Him in His house.

God has promised to meet His people there. It is their duty to go there for that specific reason. Prayer should be the chief attraction for all spiritually-minded churchgoers.

LORD GOD, I pray, that Your church would never stop meeting together. But will come together to worship You. Amen.

God Gives Freely

He who did not spare His own Son, but gave
Him up for us all – how will He not also, along
with Him, graciously give us all things?

Romans 8:32

What a basis we have here for prayer and faith!
The promise to give us *"all things"* is backed by the
fact that God gave His one and only Son for our
redemption.

We can therefore come to God with our requests
and ask boldly and confidently.

The more faith we have in God to supply our
needs, the more grace He will give us and we will see
His glory. When you pray, believe that God is able to
freely give you all things.

FATHER GOD, I believe that You are able to
freely give me all good things. Thank You for Your
mercy and grace. Amen.

Christ's Intercession

Pray continually.

1 Thessalonians 5:17

How enthroned, magnificent, and royal is the intercession of our Lord Jesus Christ at His Father's right hand in heaven!

The benefits of His intercession flow to us through our intercessions. Our intercession should connect to a plan greater than our own – God's plan. His business and His life are to pray. Our business and our lives ought to be to pray too and failure in our intercession affects the fruit of His intercession.

Lazy, heartless, feeble, and indifferent praying hinders the effects of Christ's praying on our behalf.

★　★　★

LORD GOD, just like Jesus, I want the business of my life to be to pray. Please guide me through the power of Your Spirit. Amen.